Discount Graffiti

Black Book

Kenneth Andre "Search" Brown Sr © 2018

Amazon Self Publishing

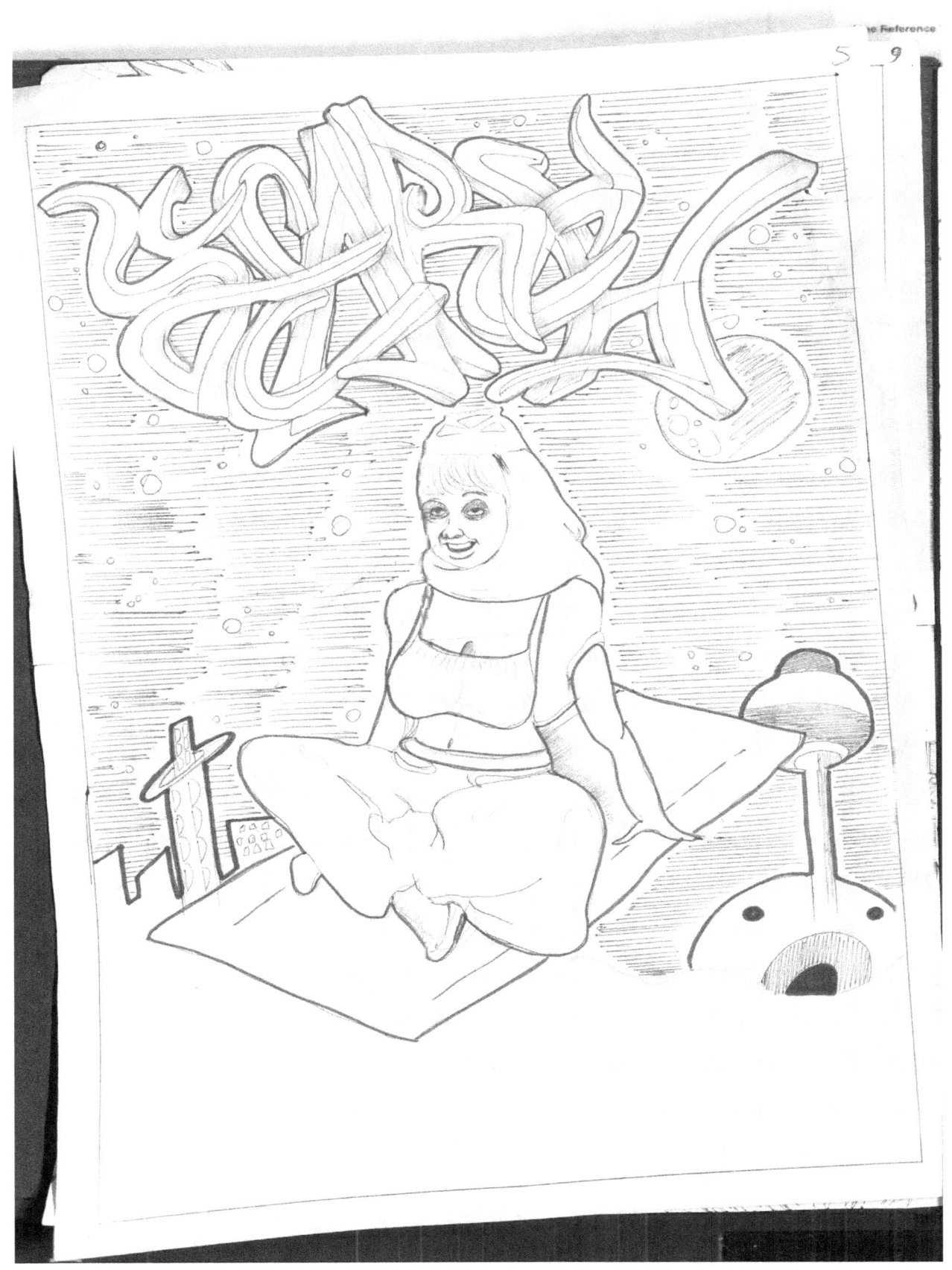

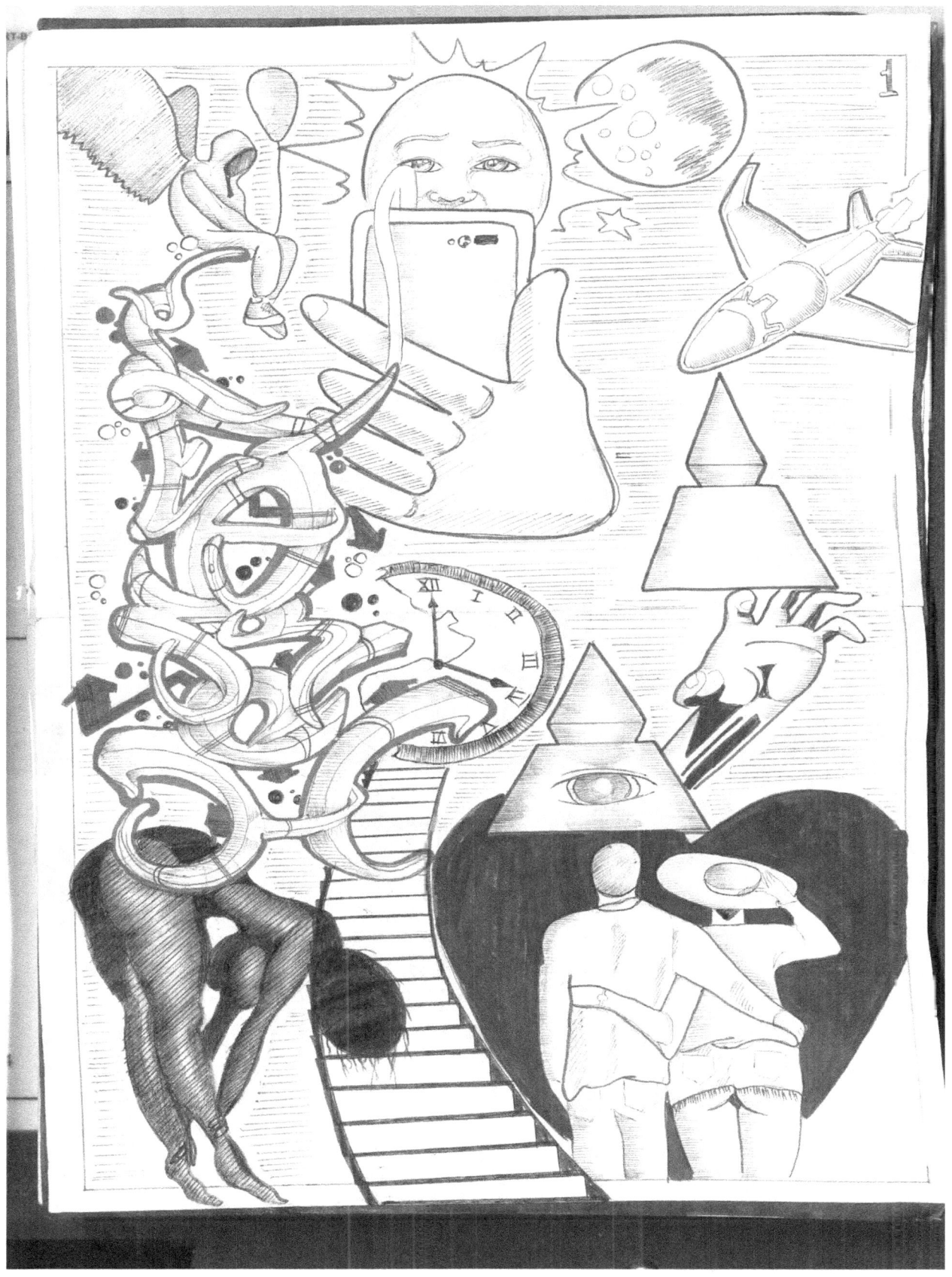

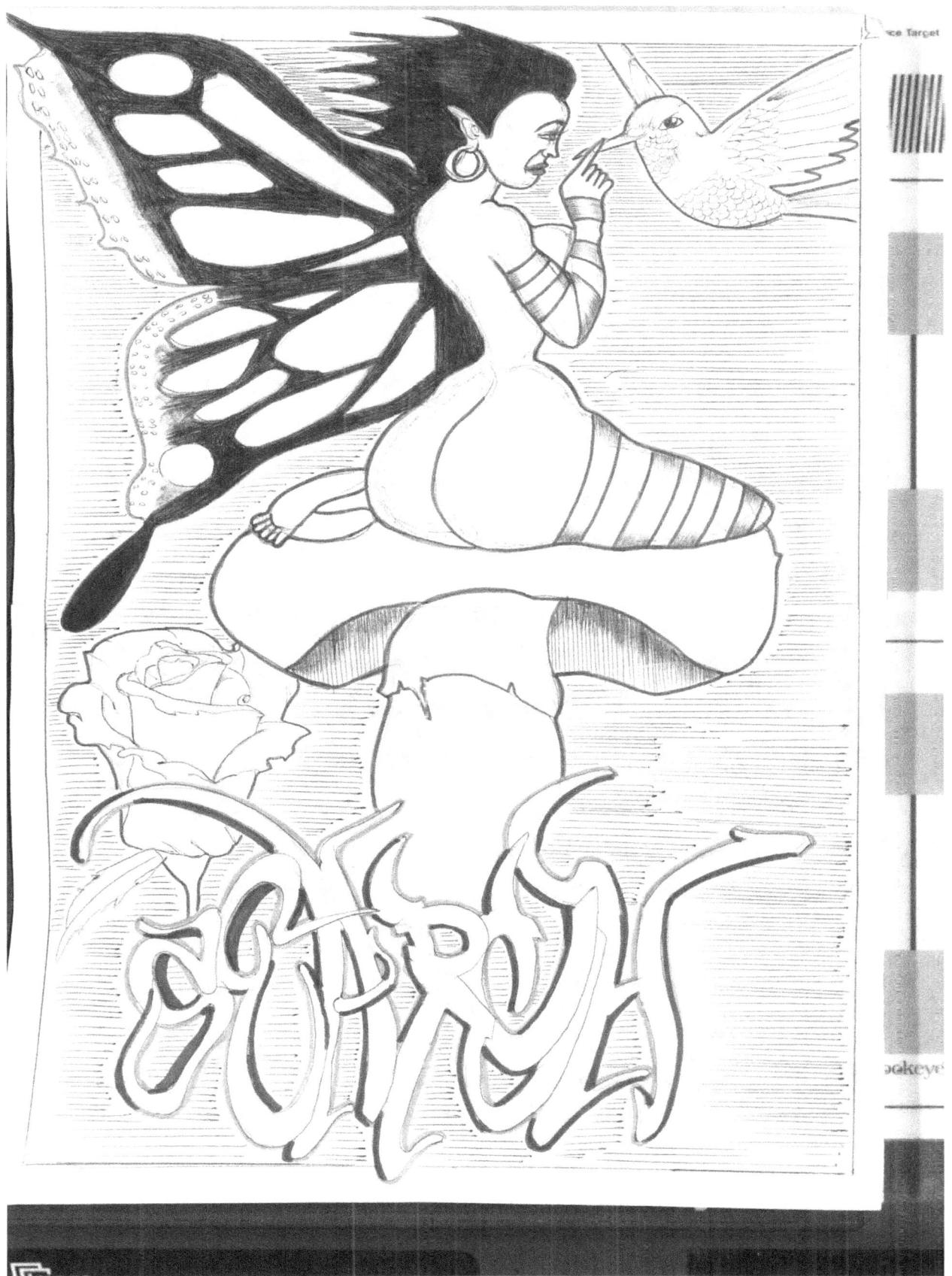

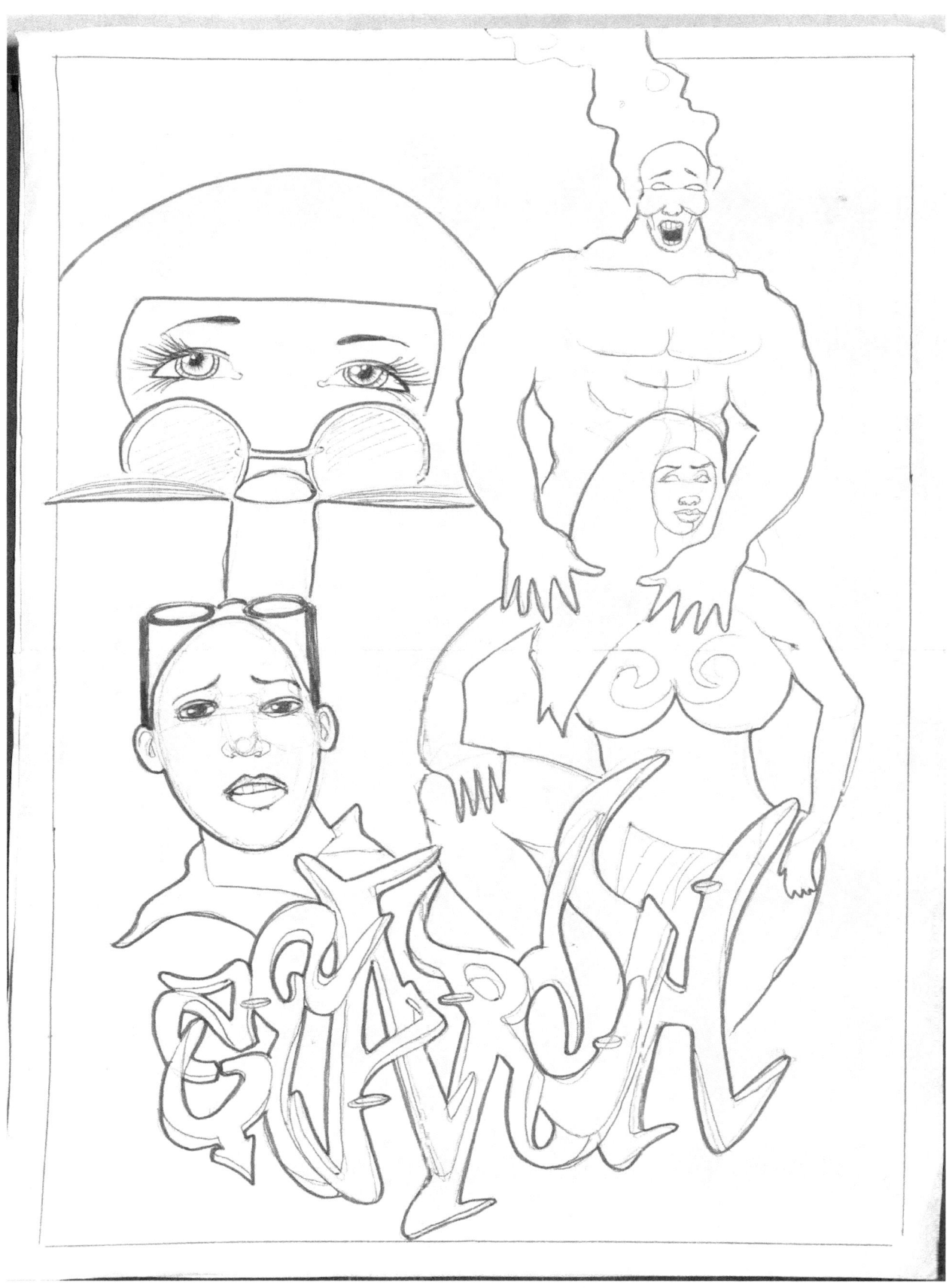

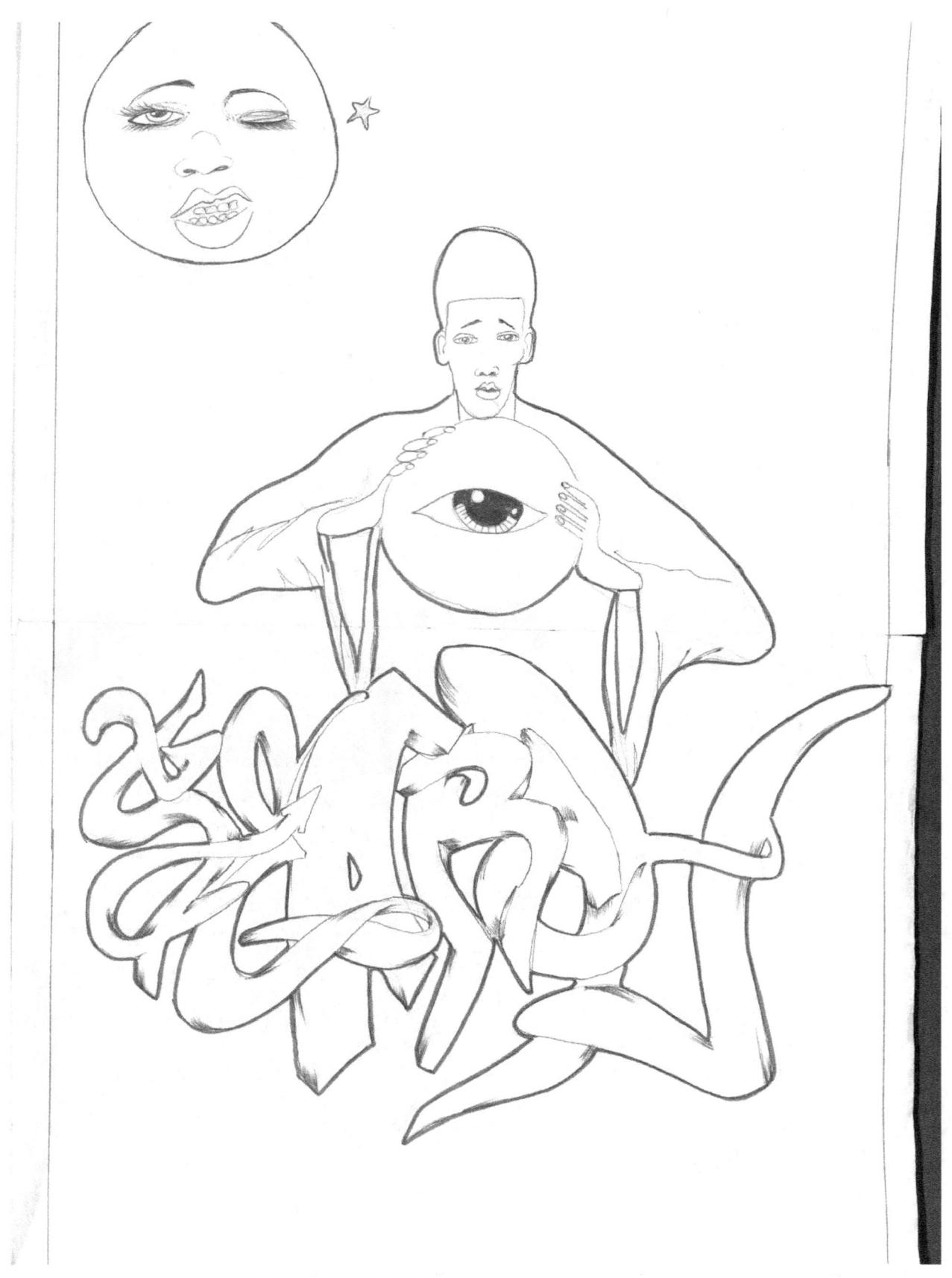

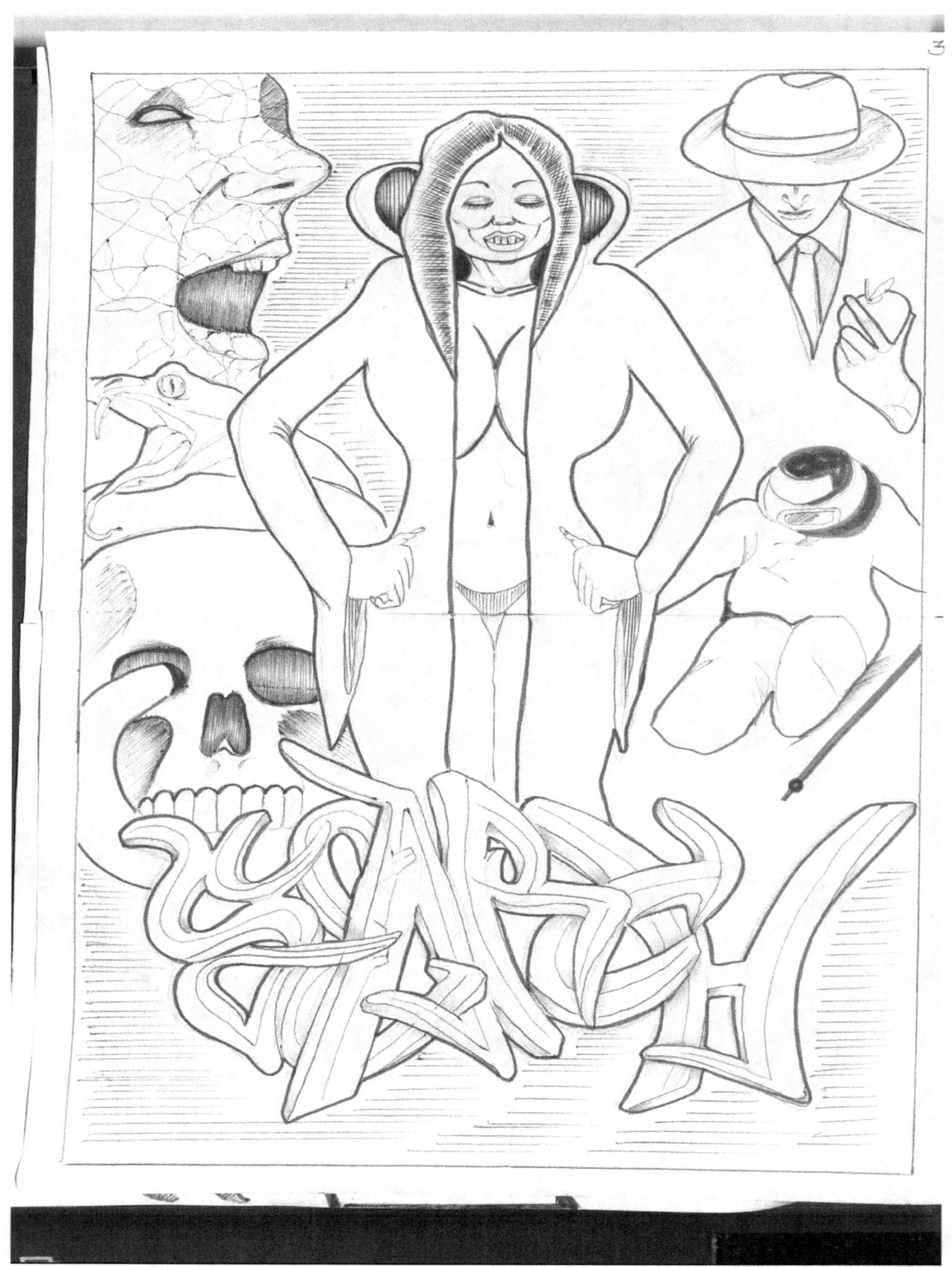

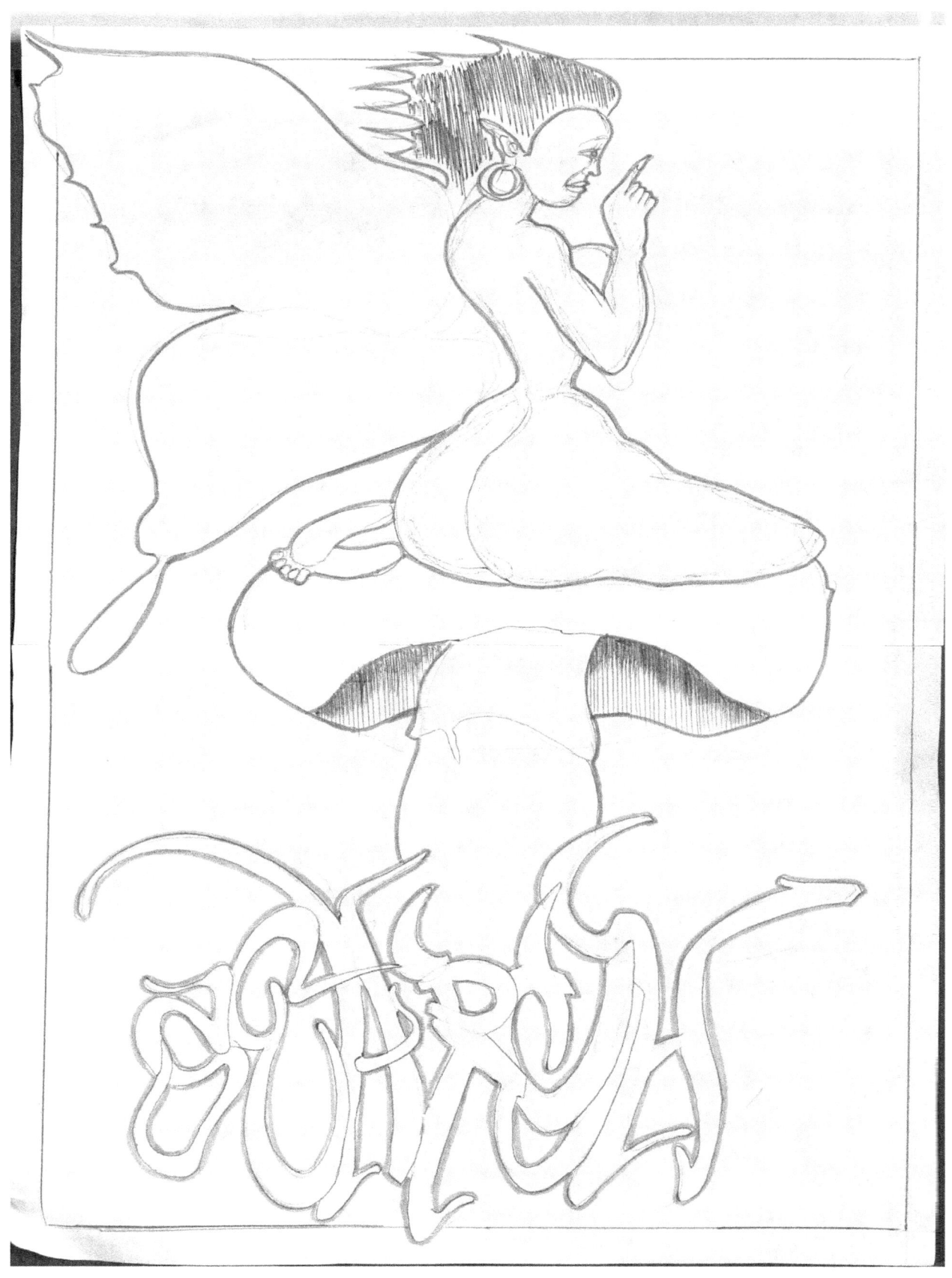

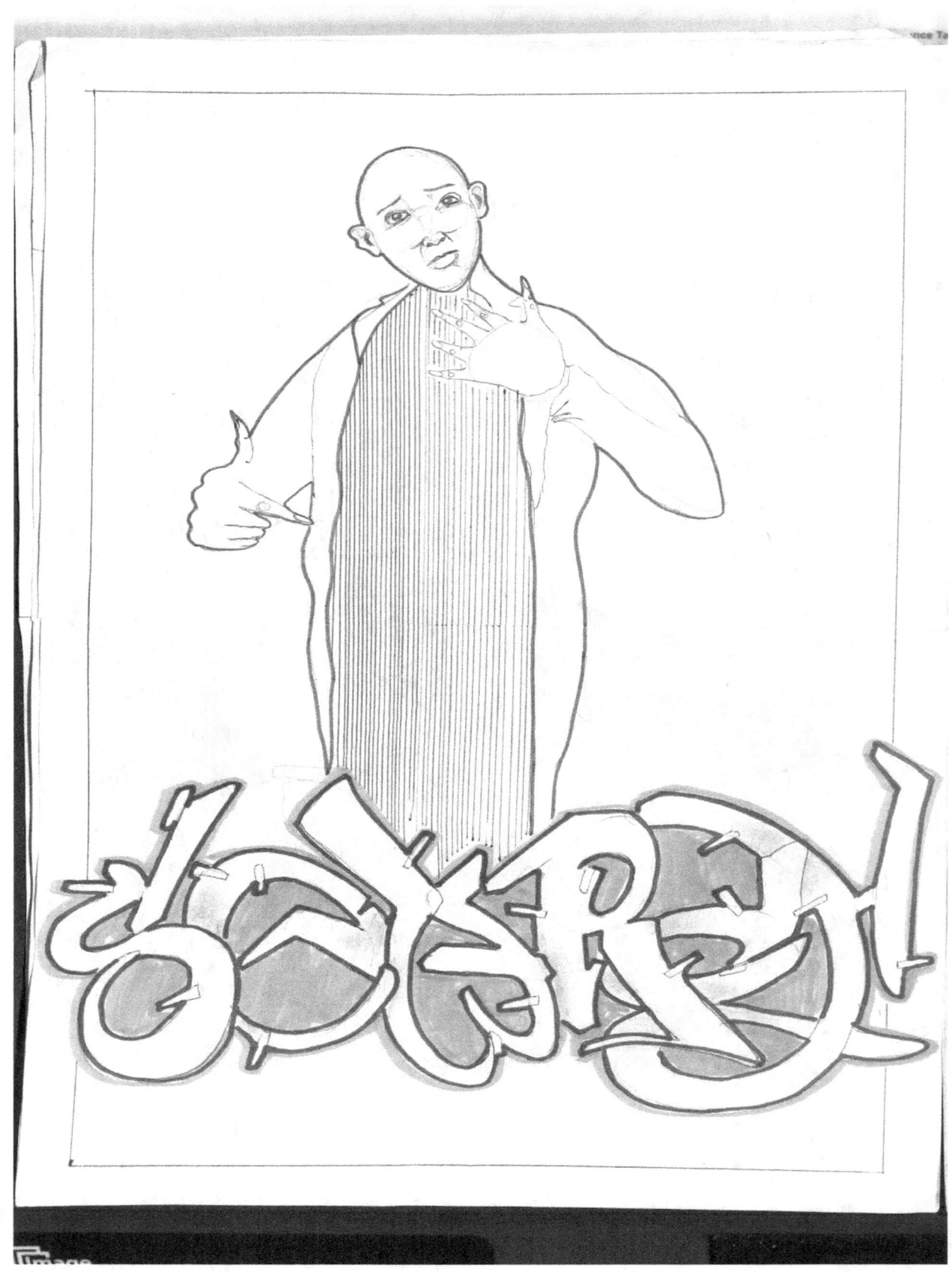

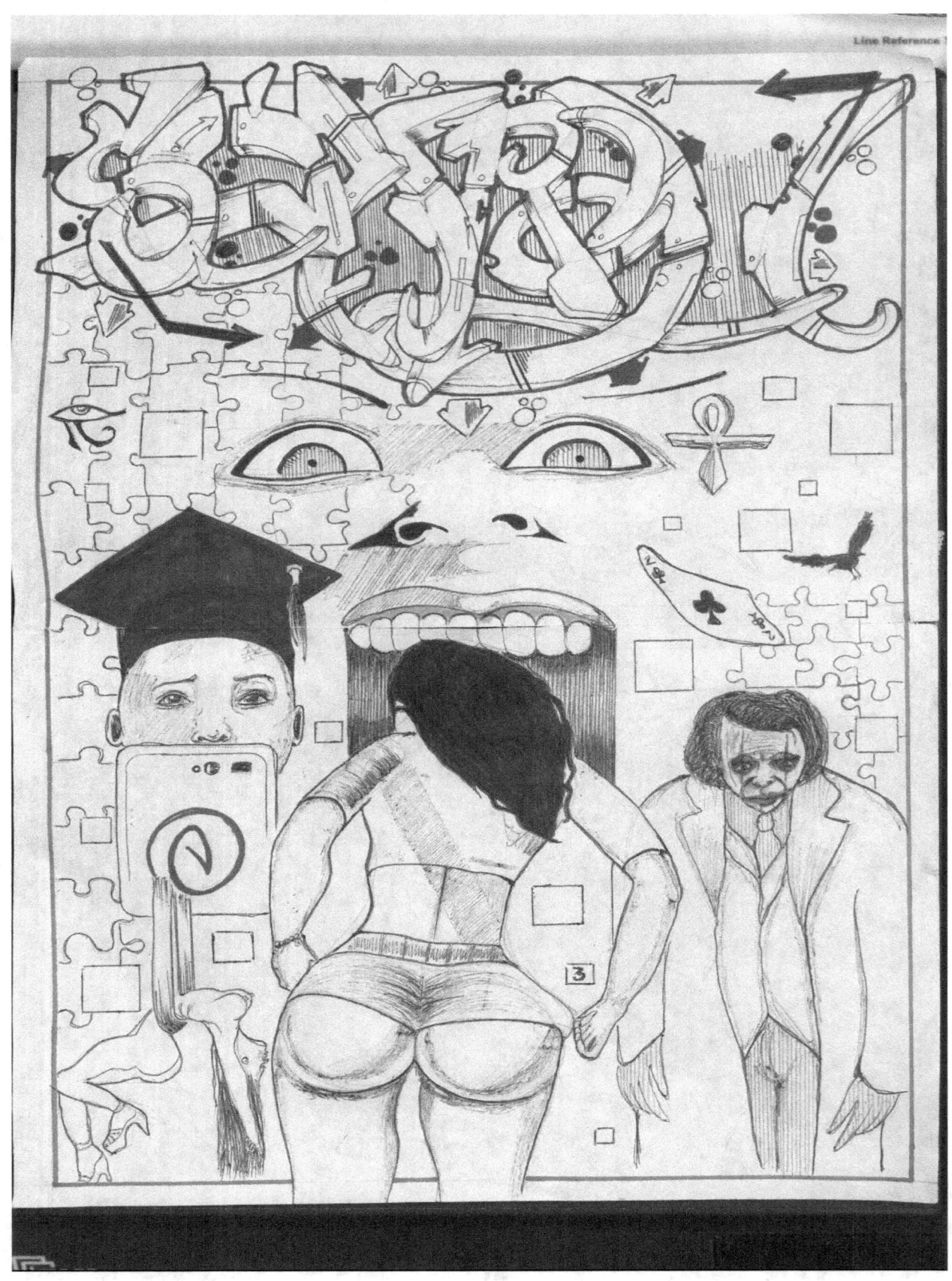

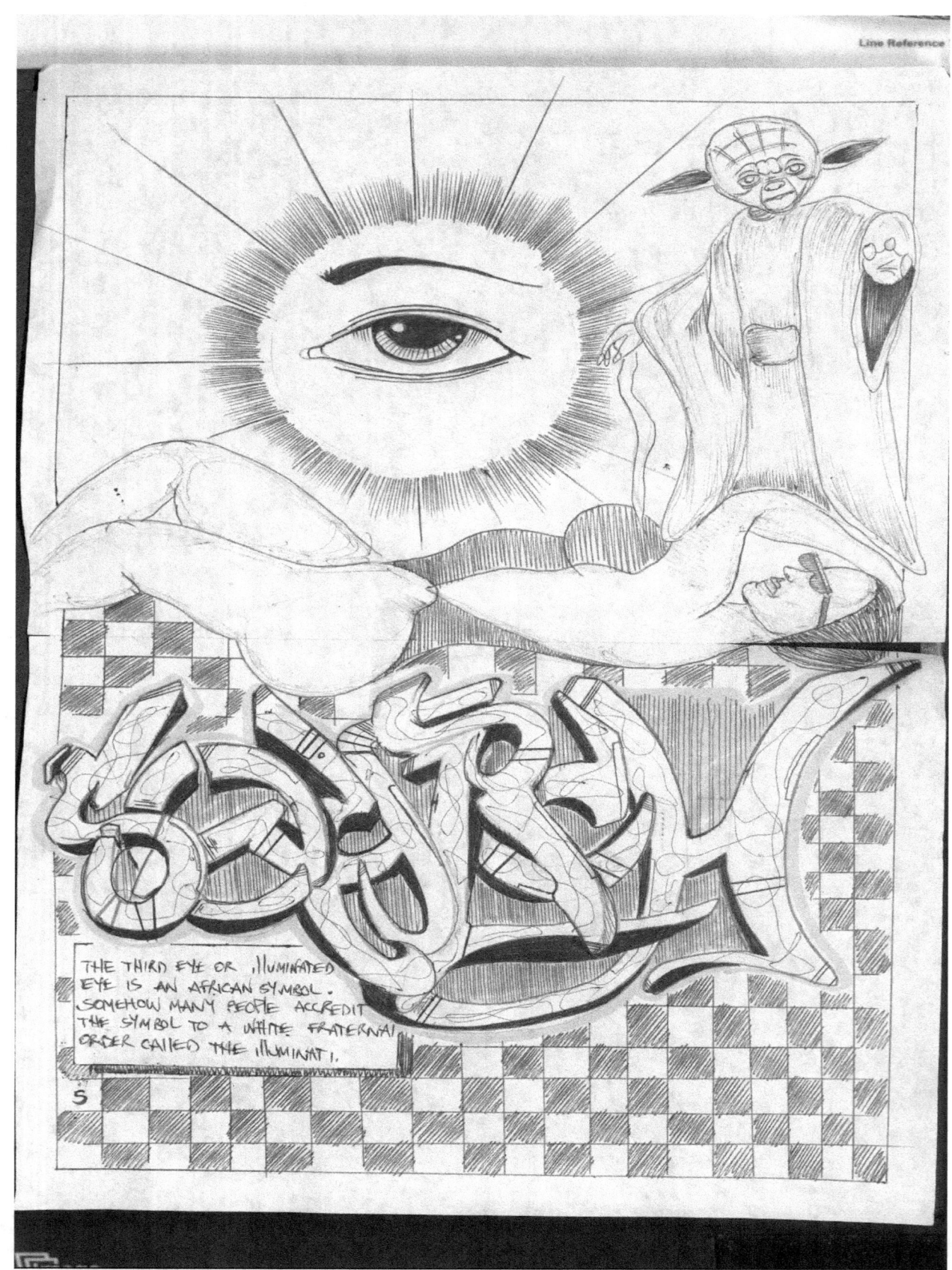

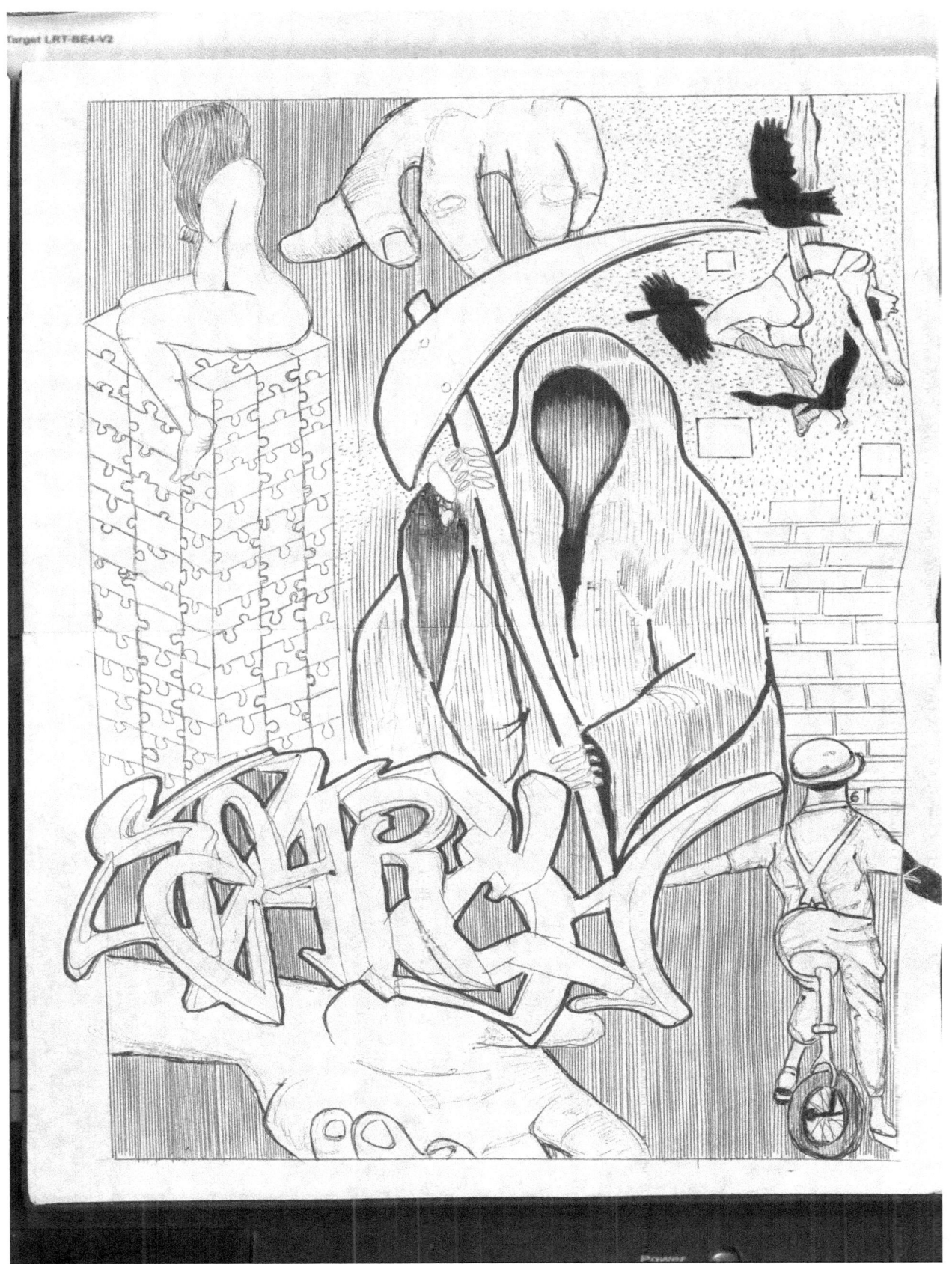

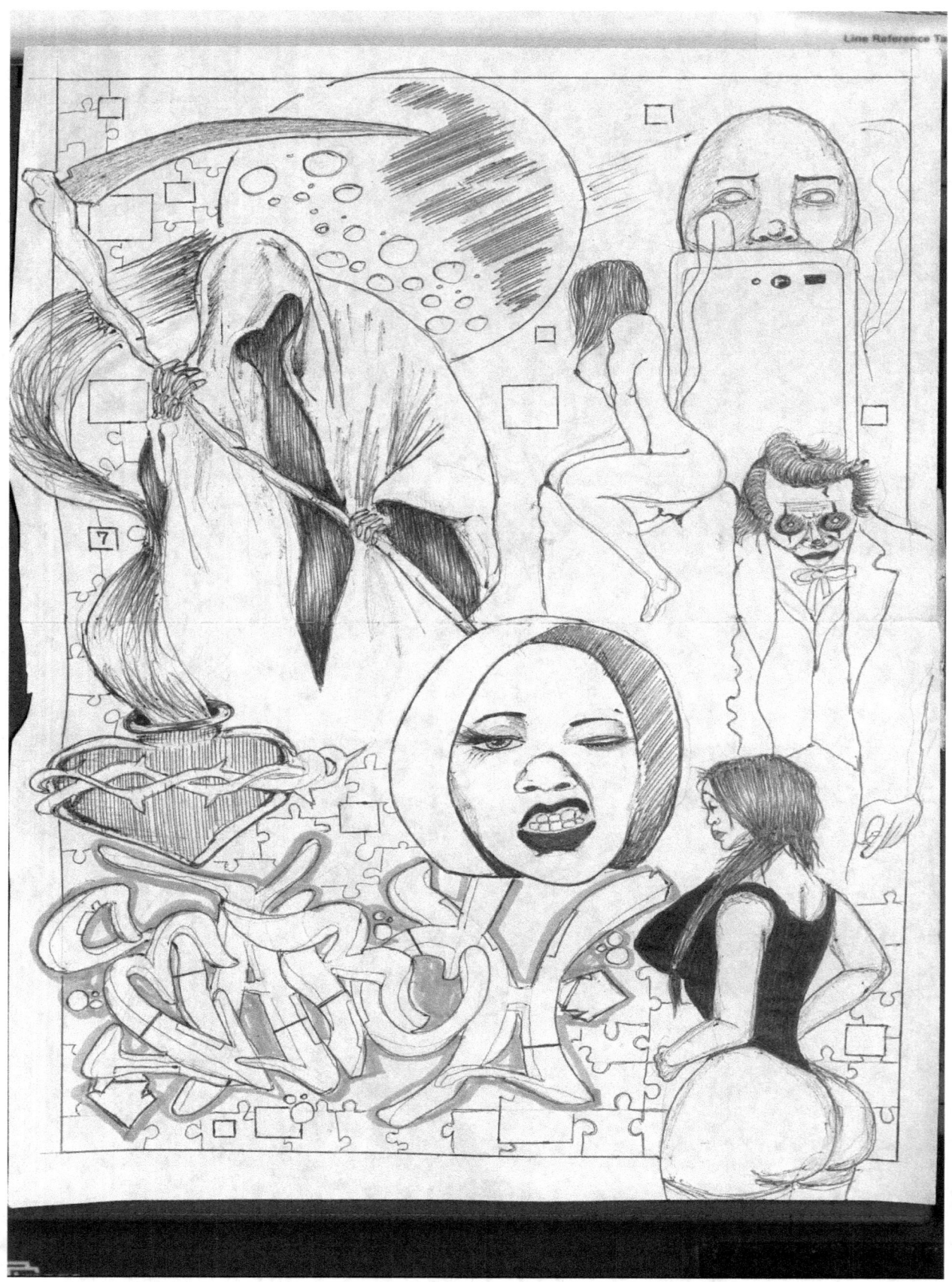

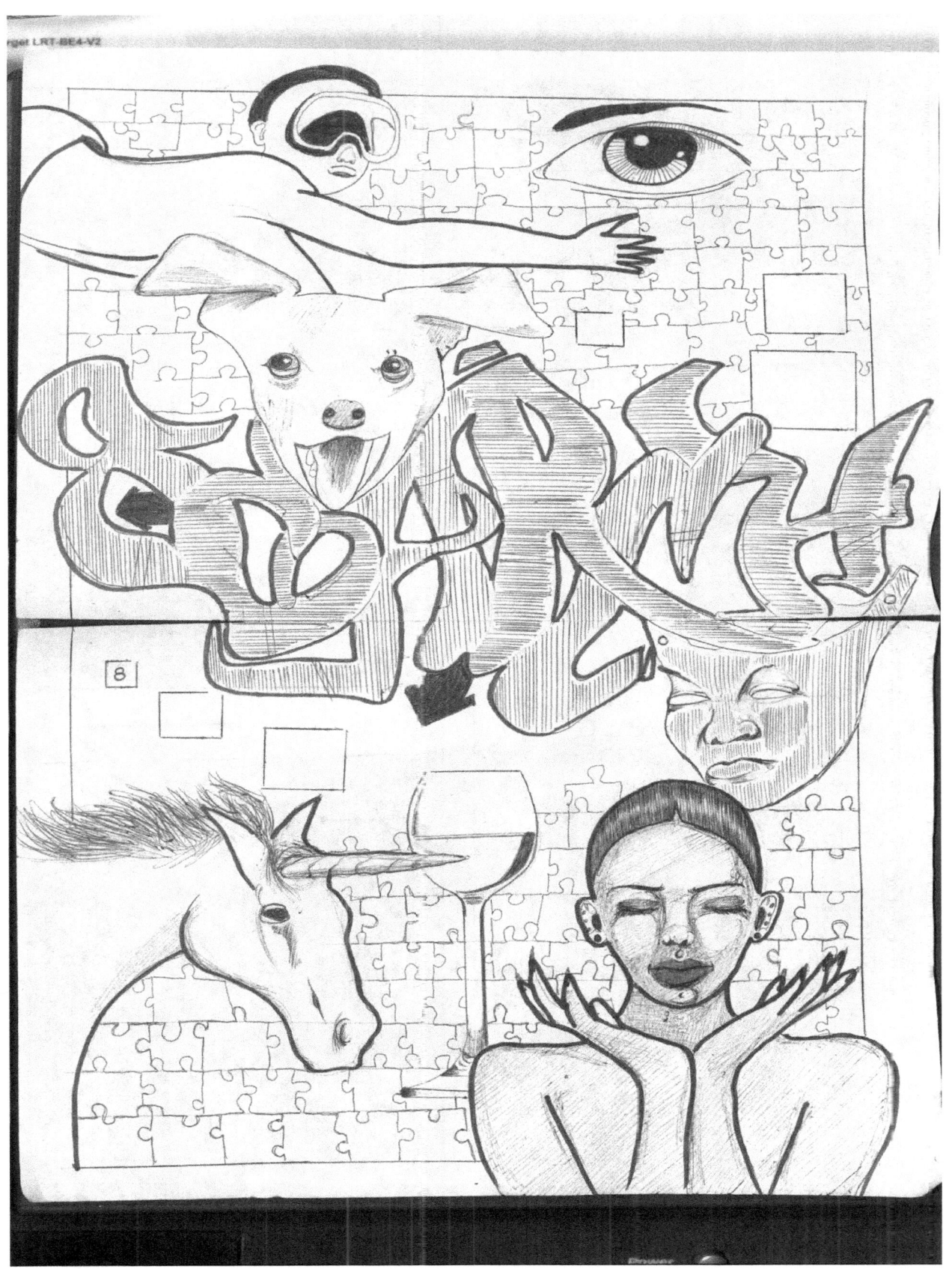

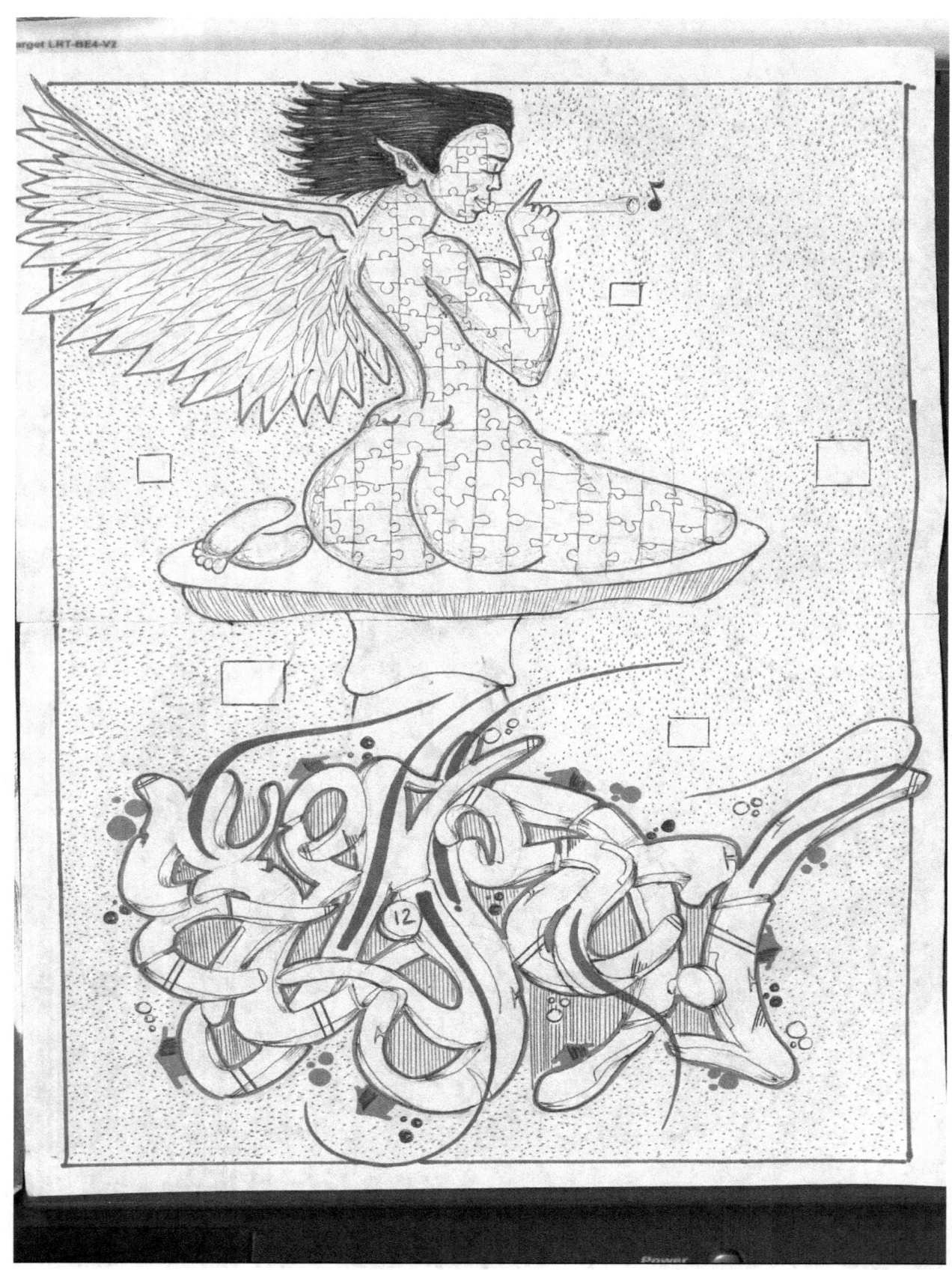

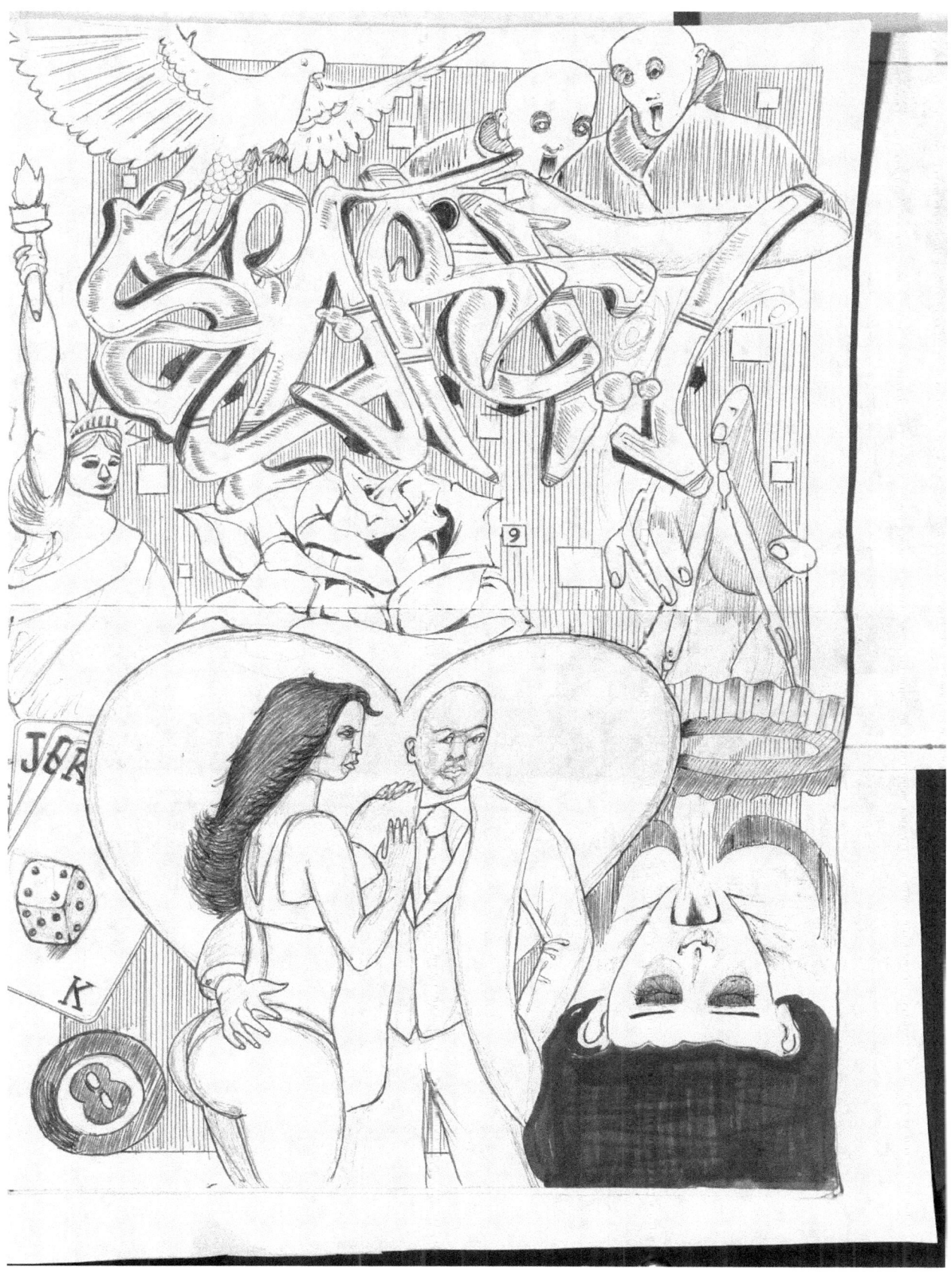

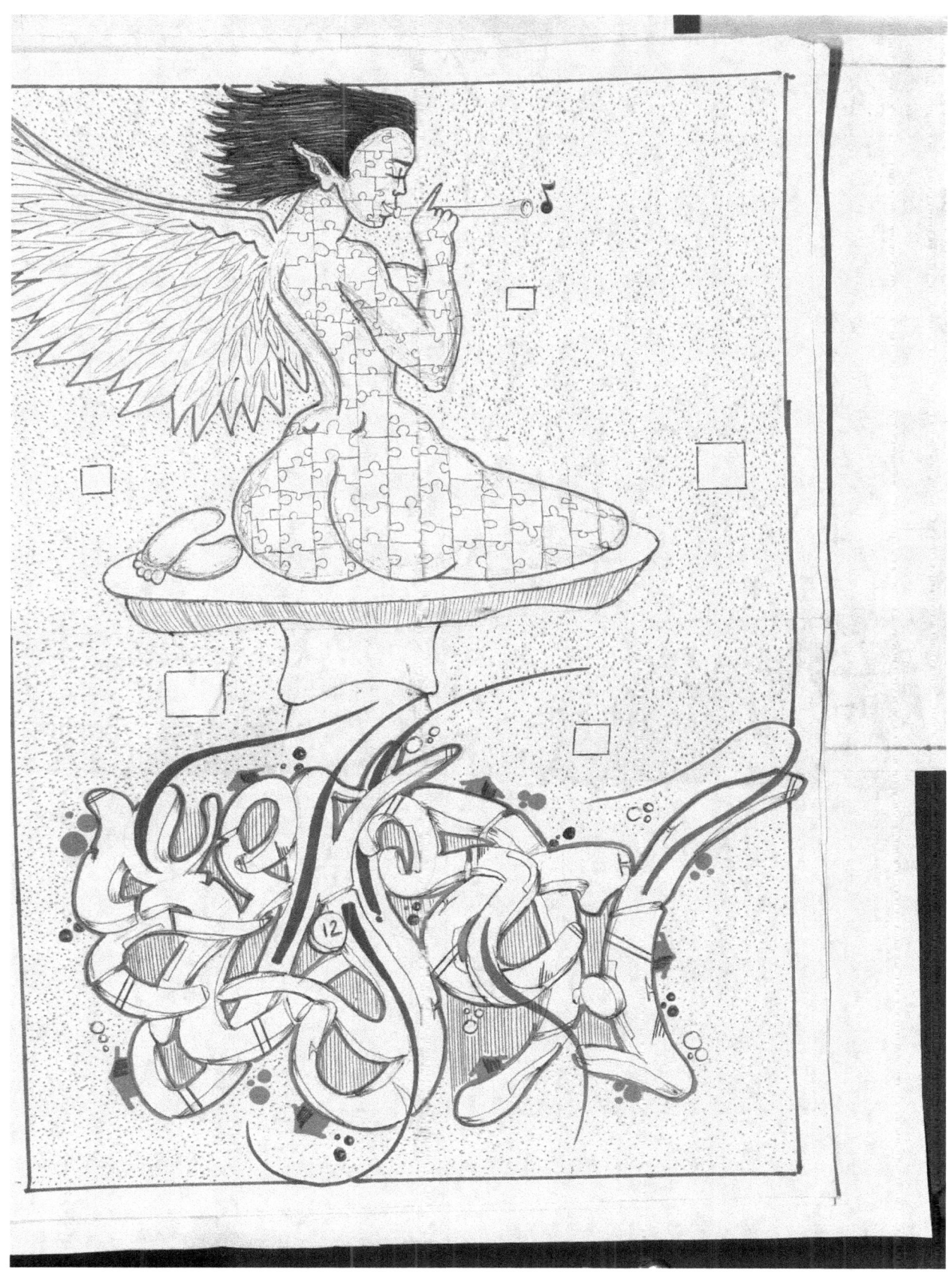

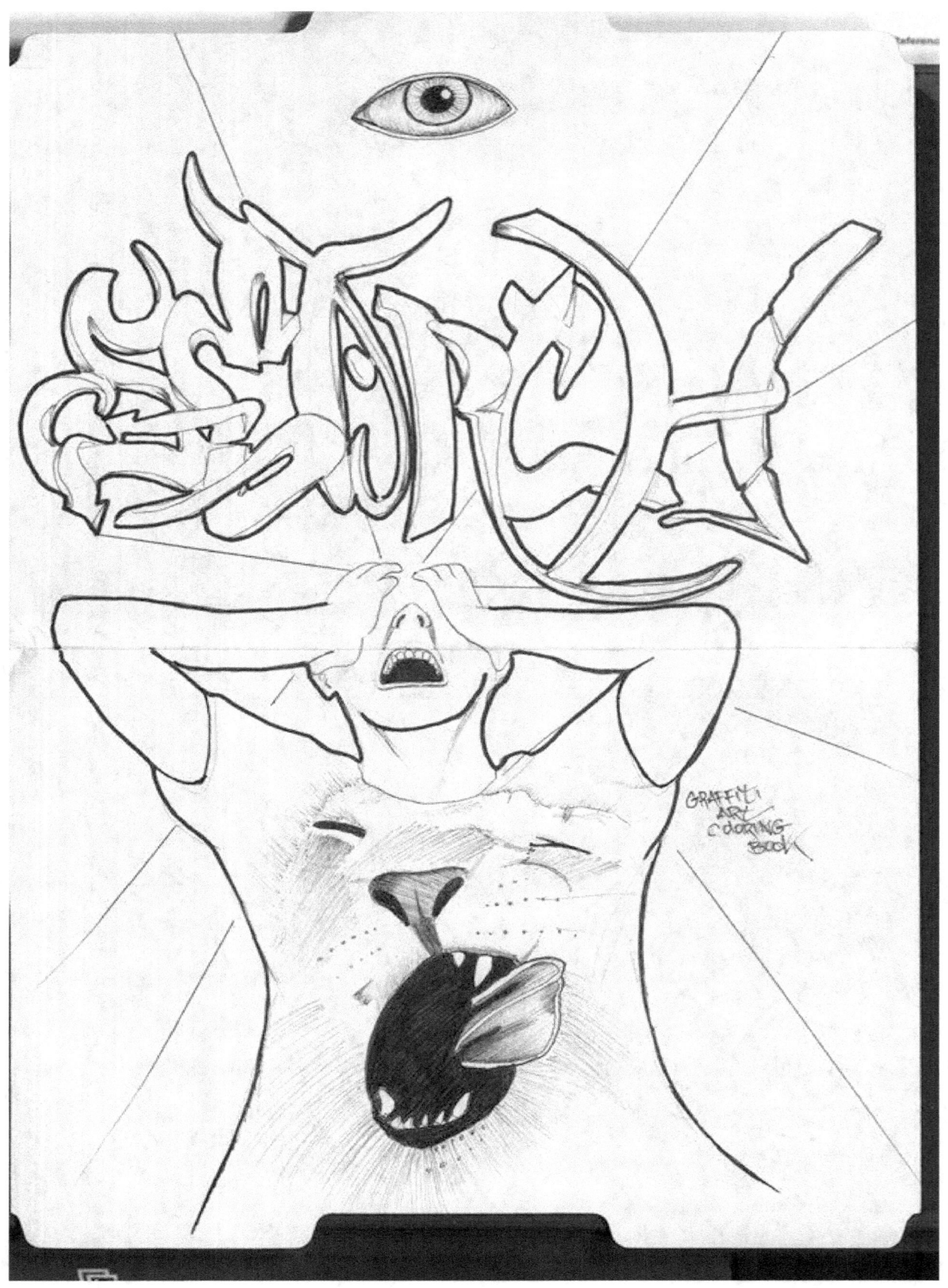

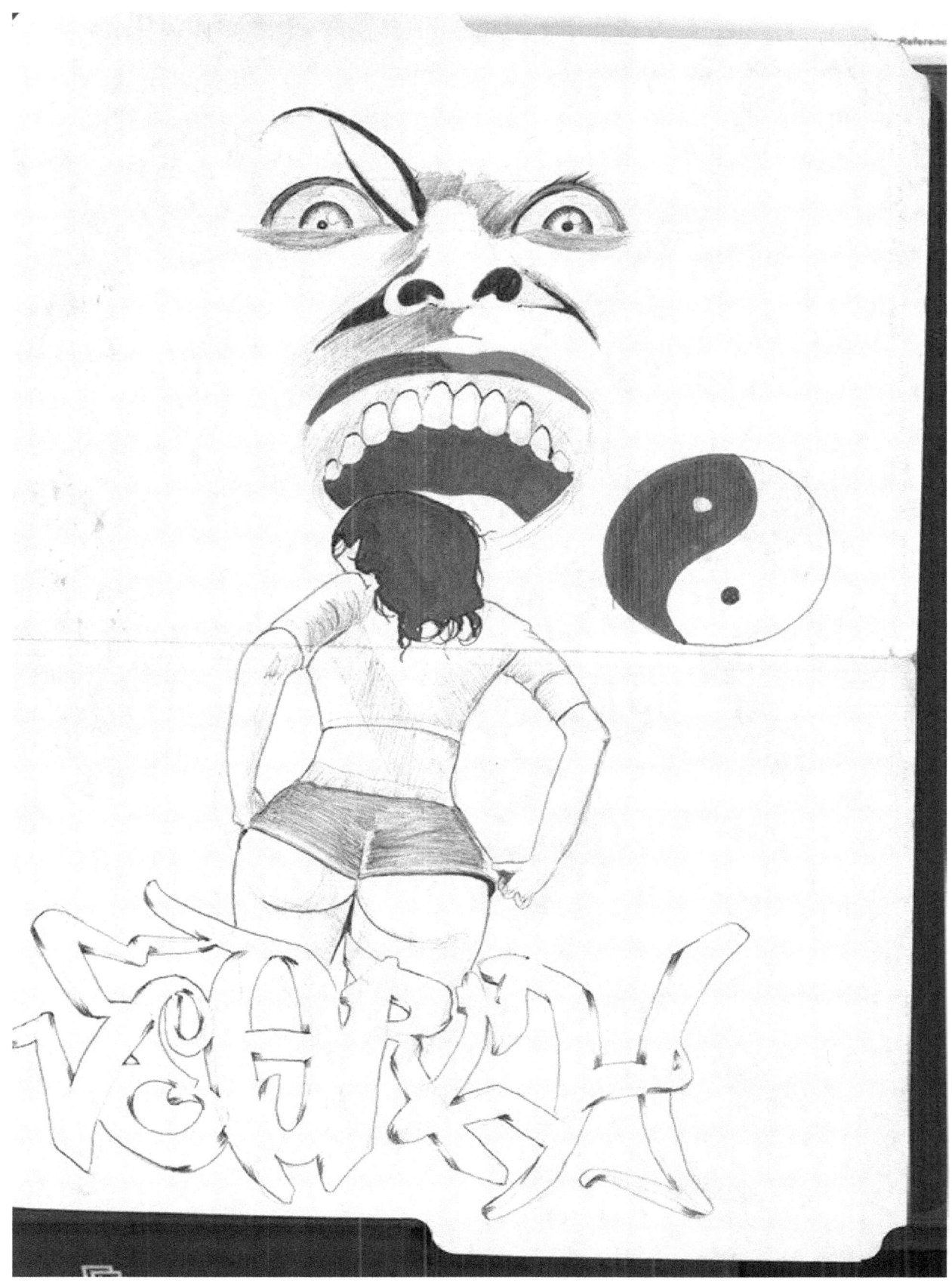

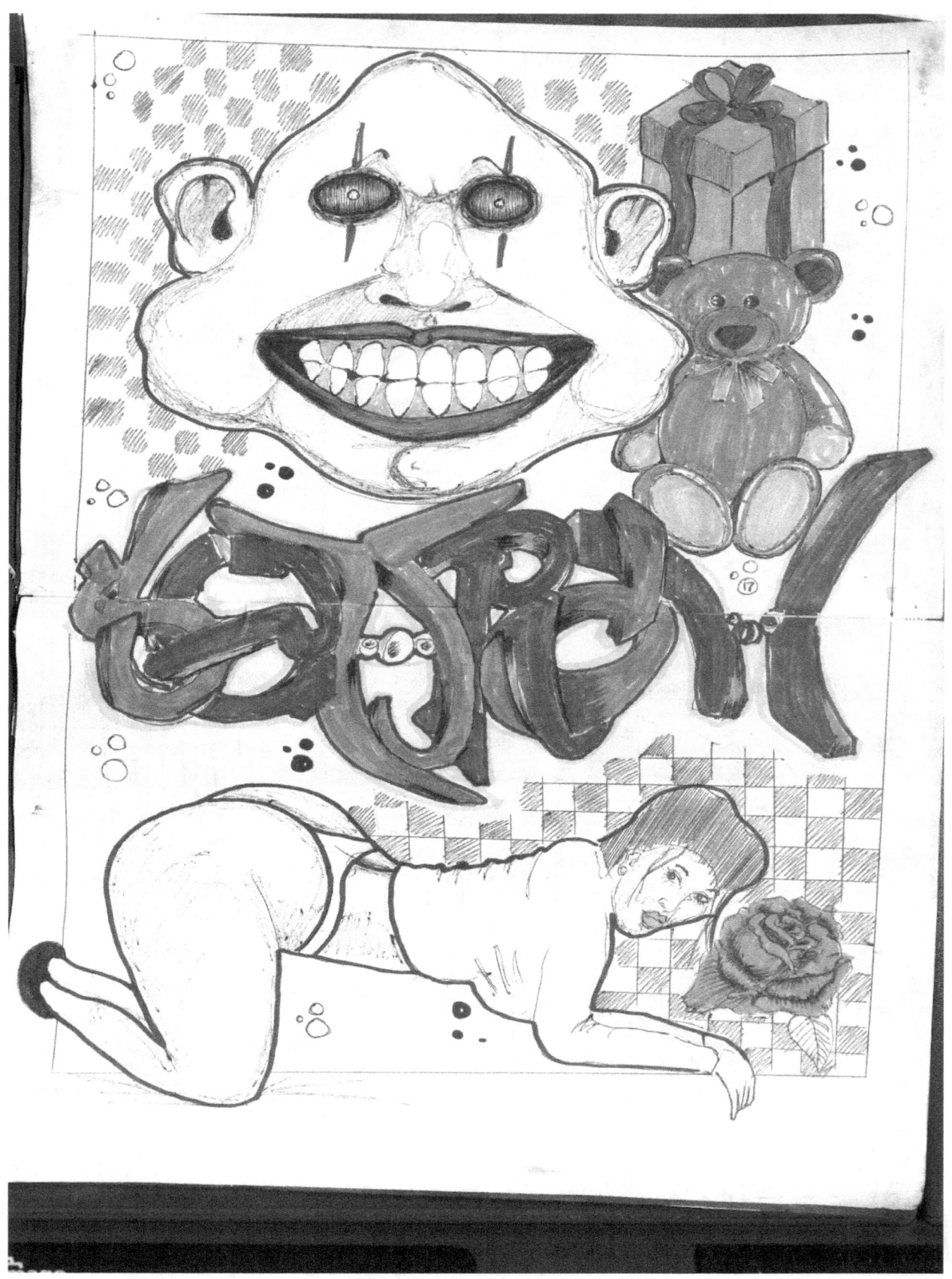

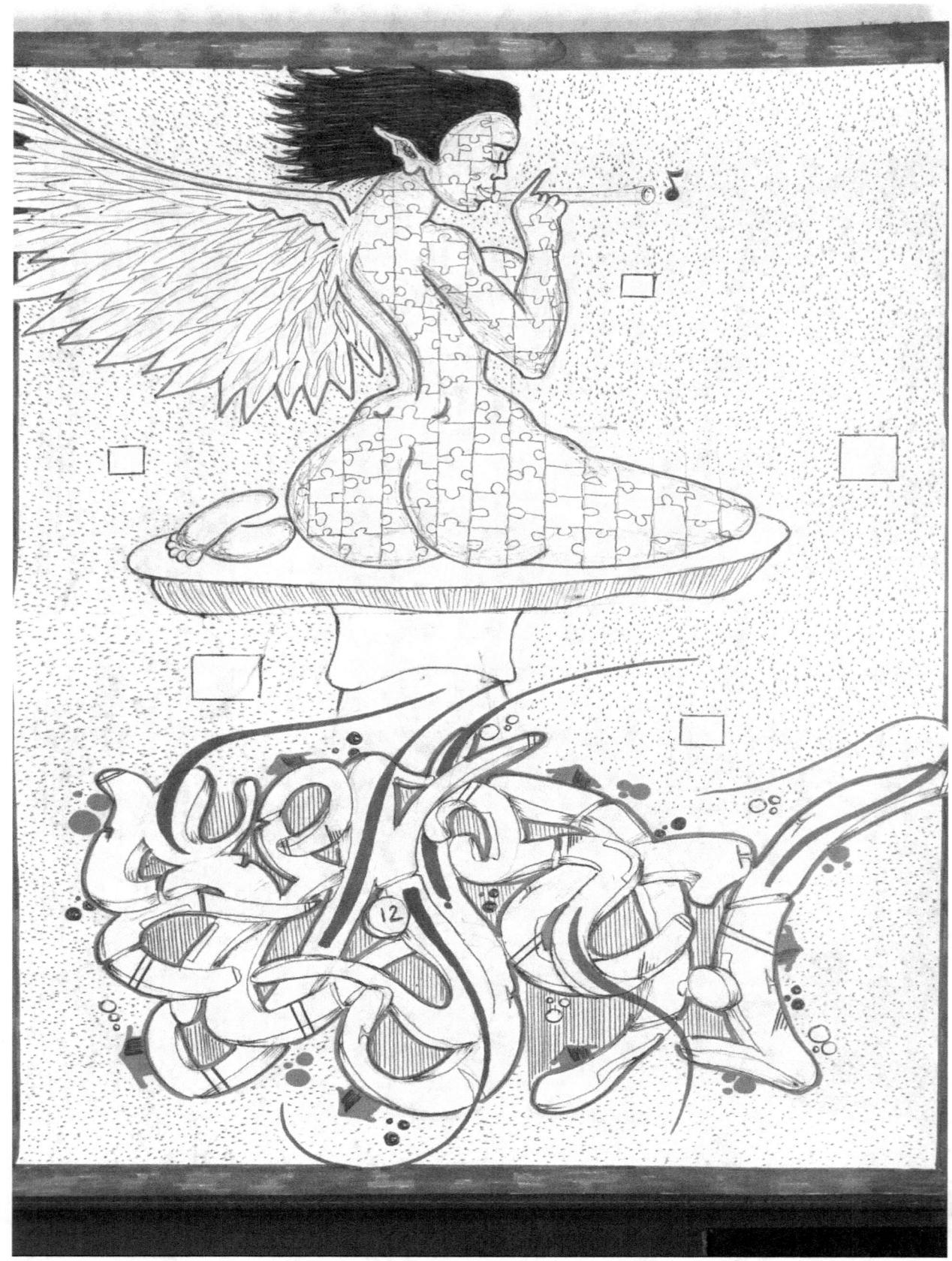

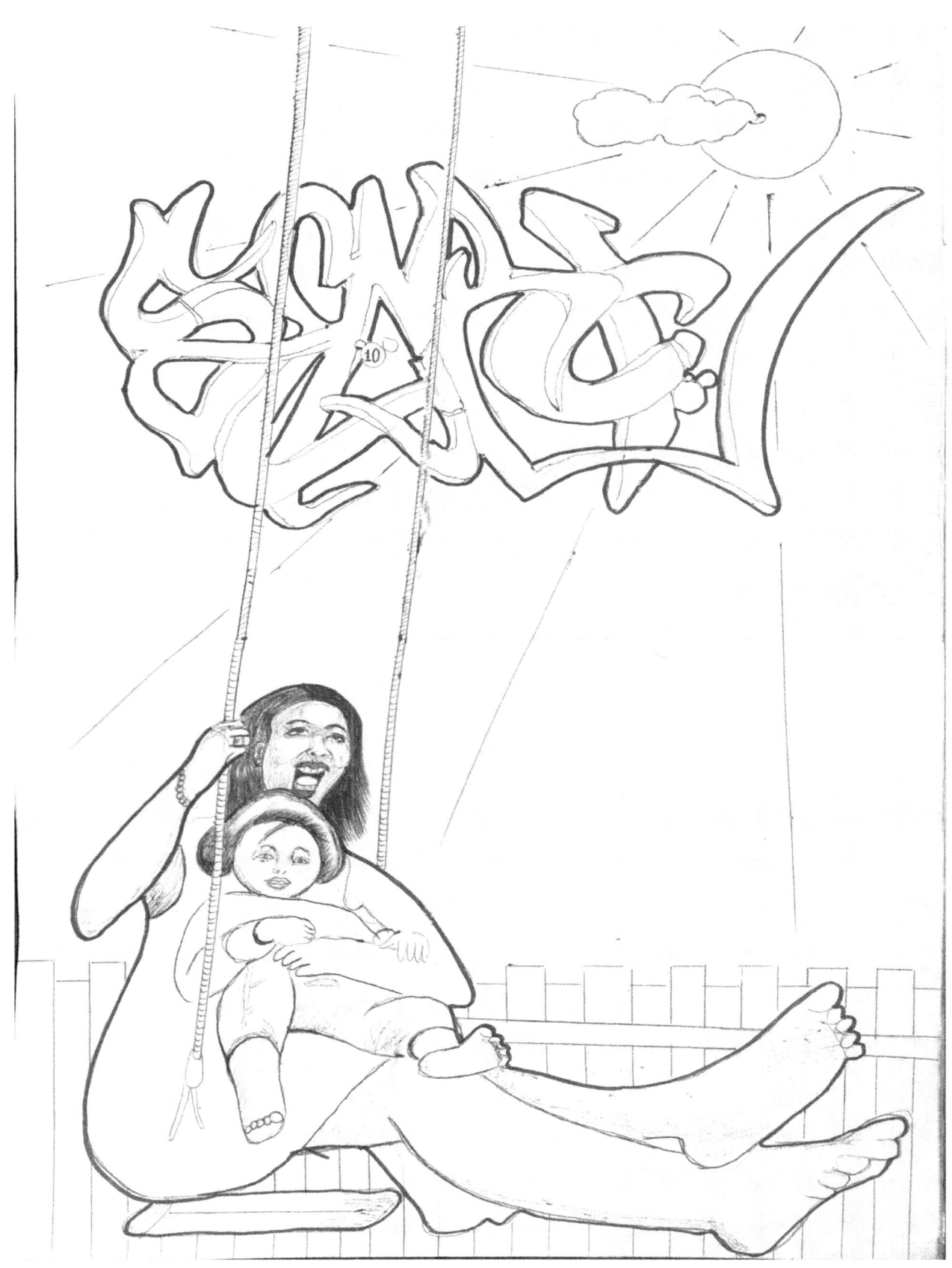

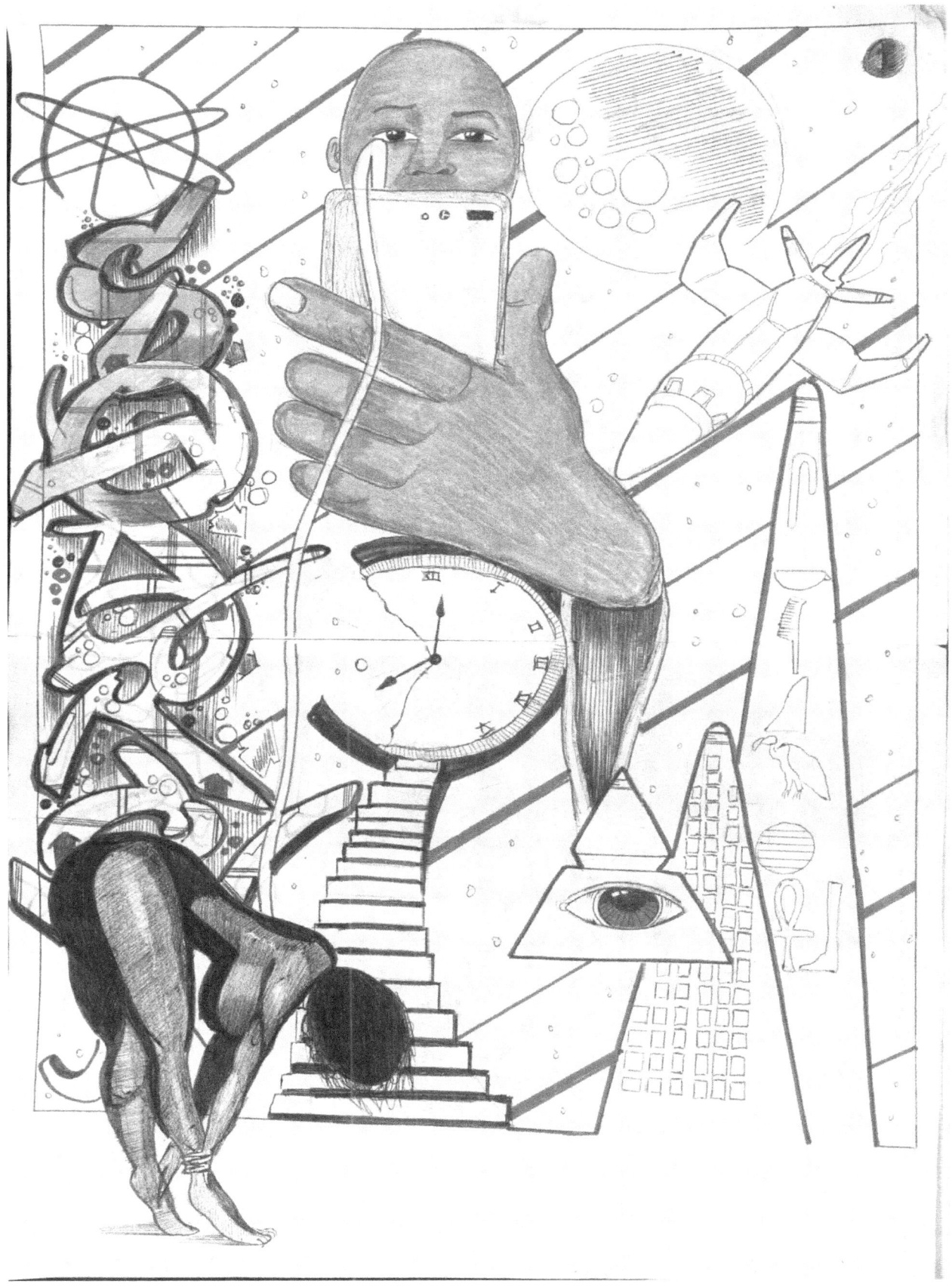

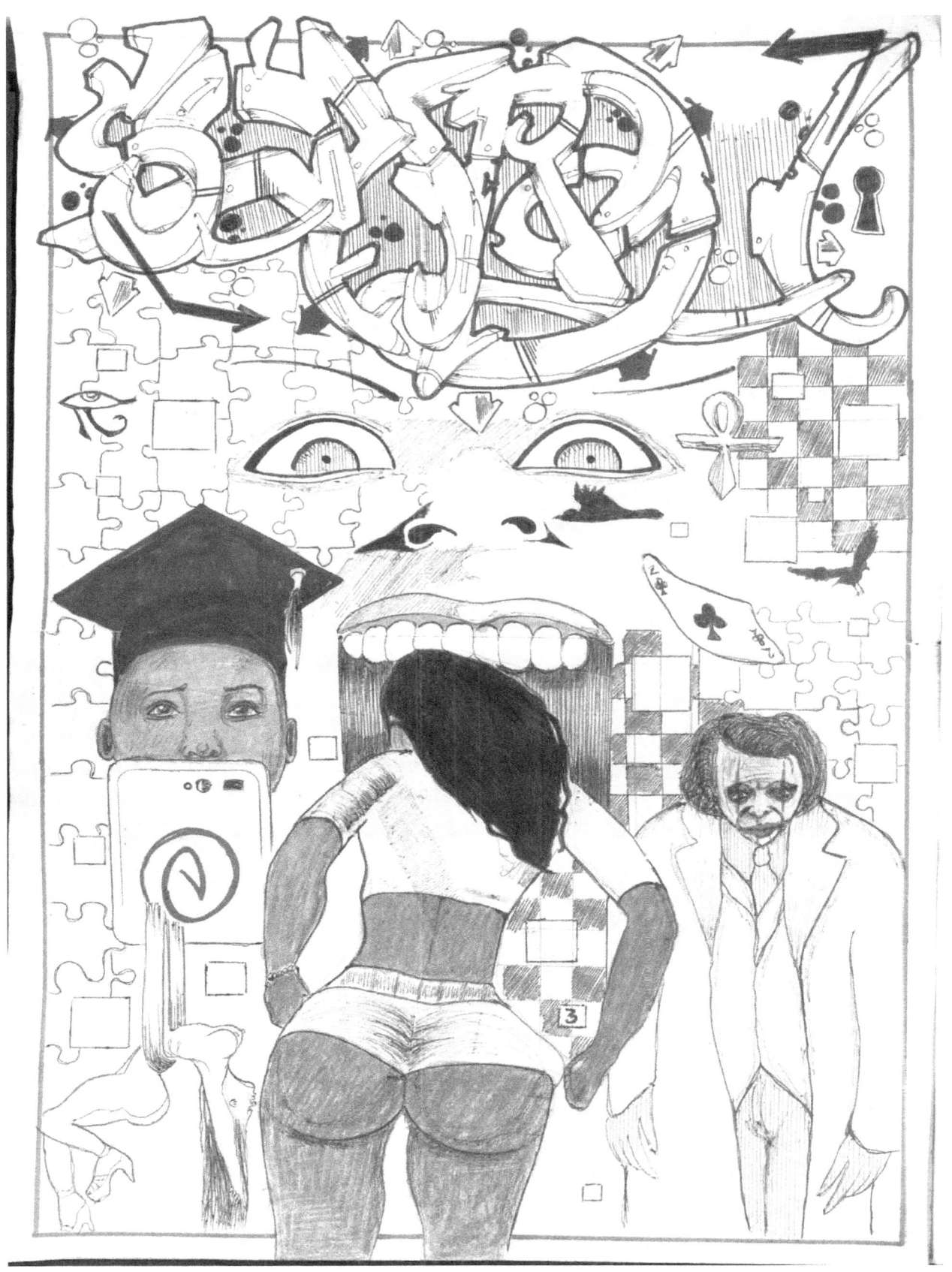

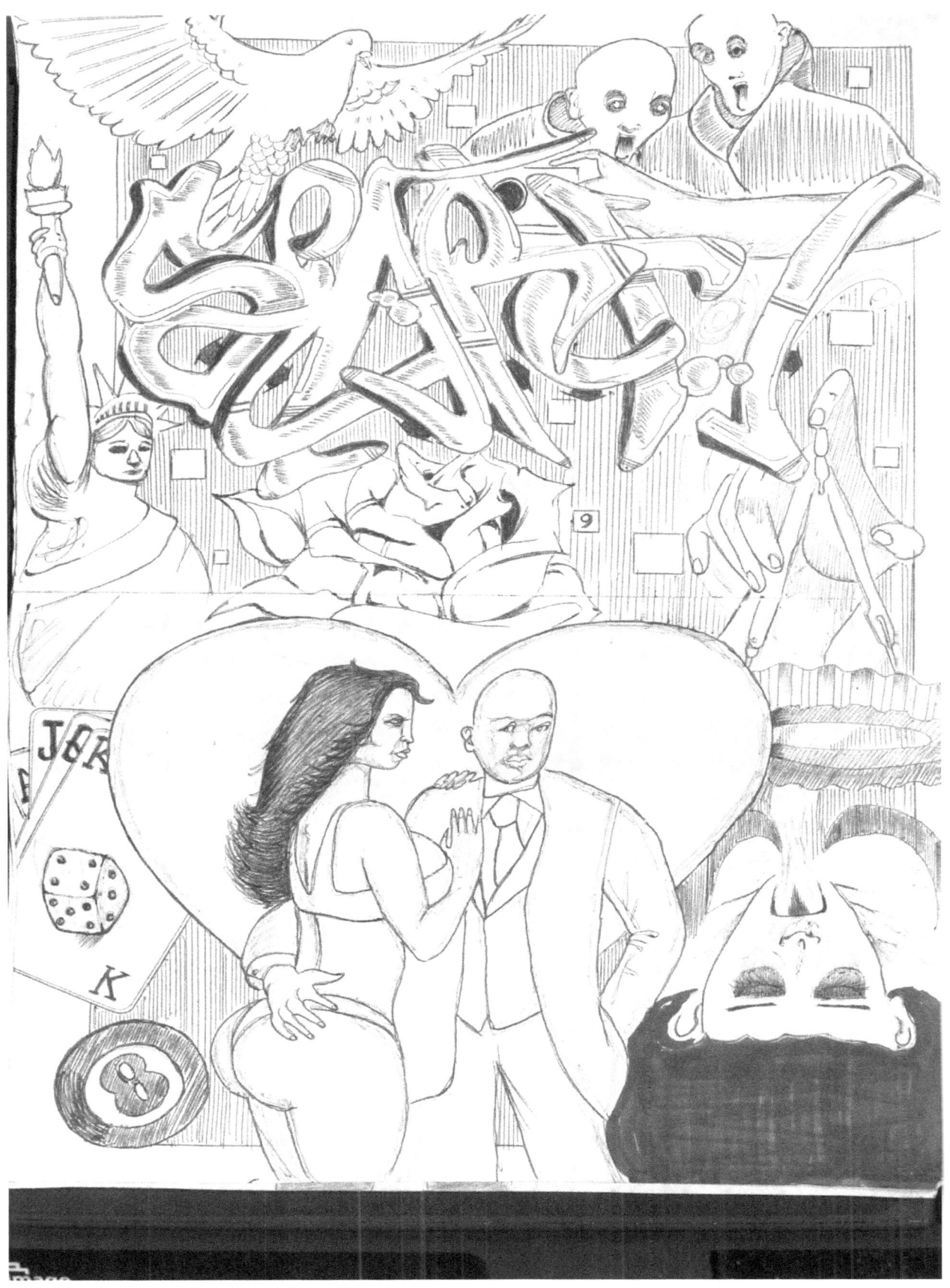

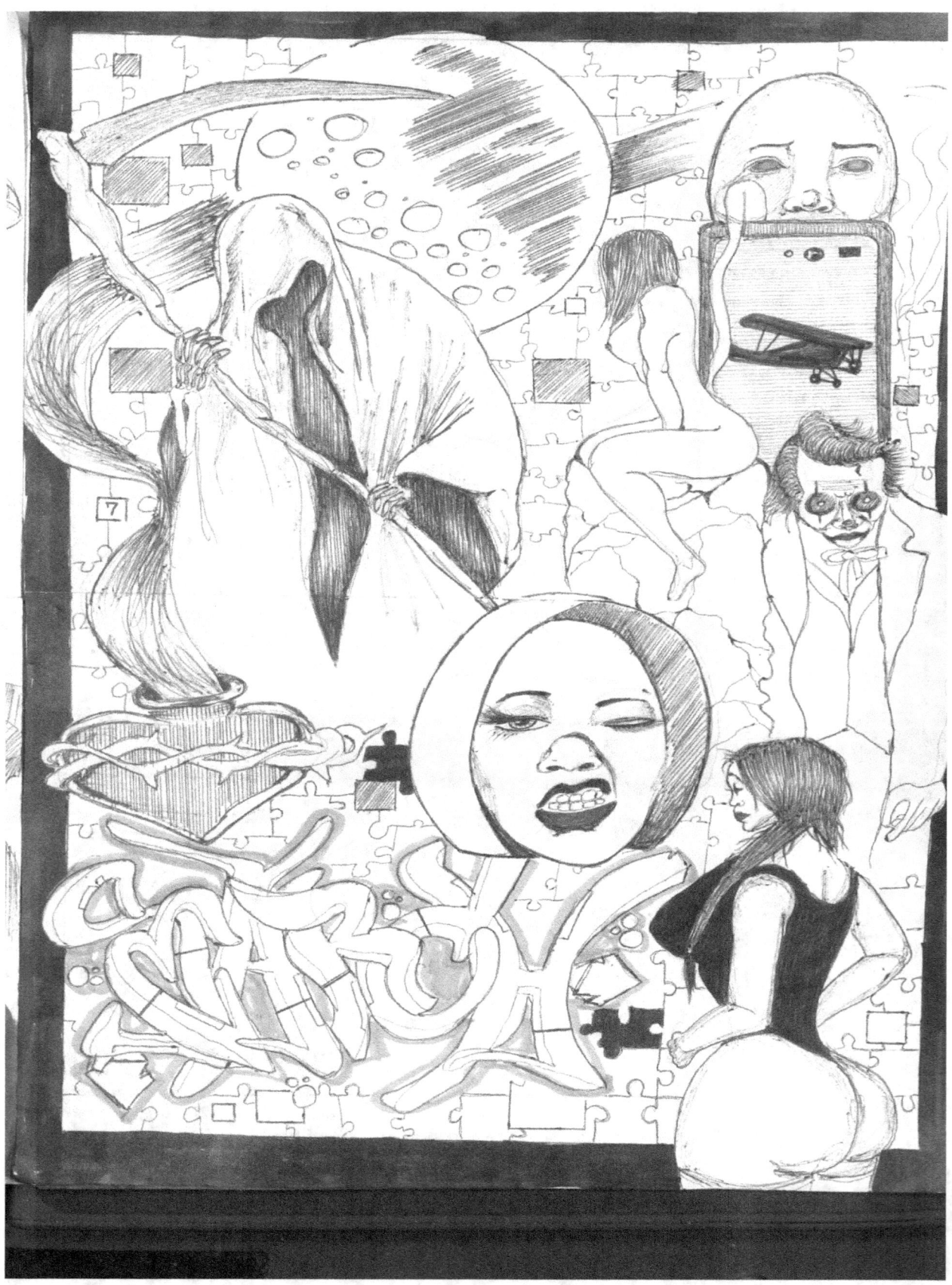

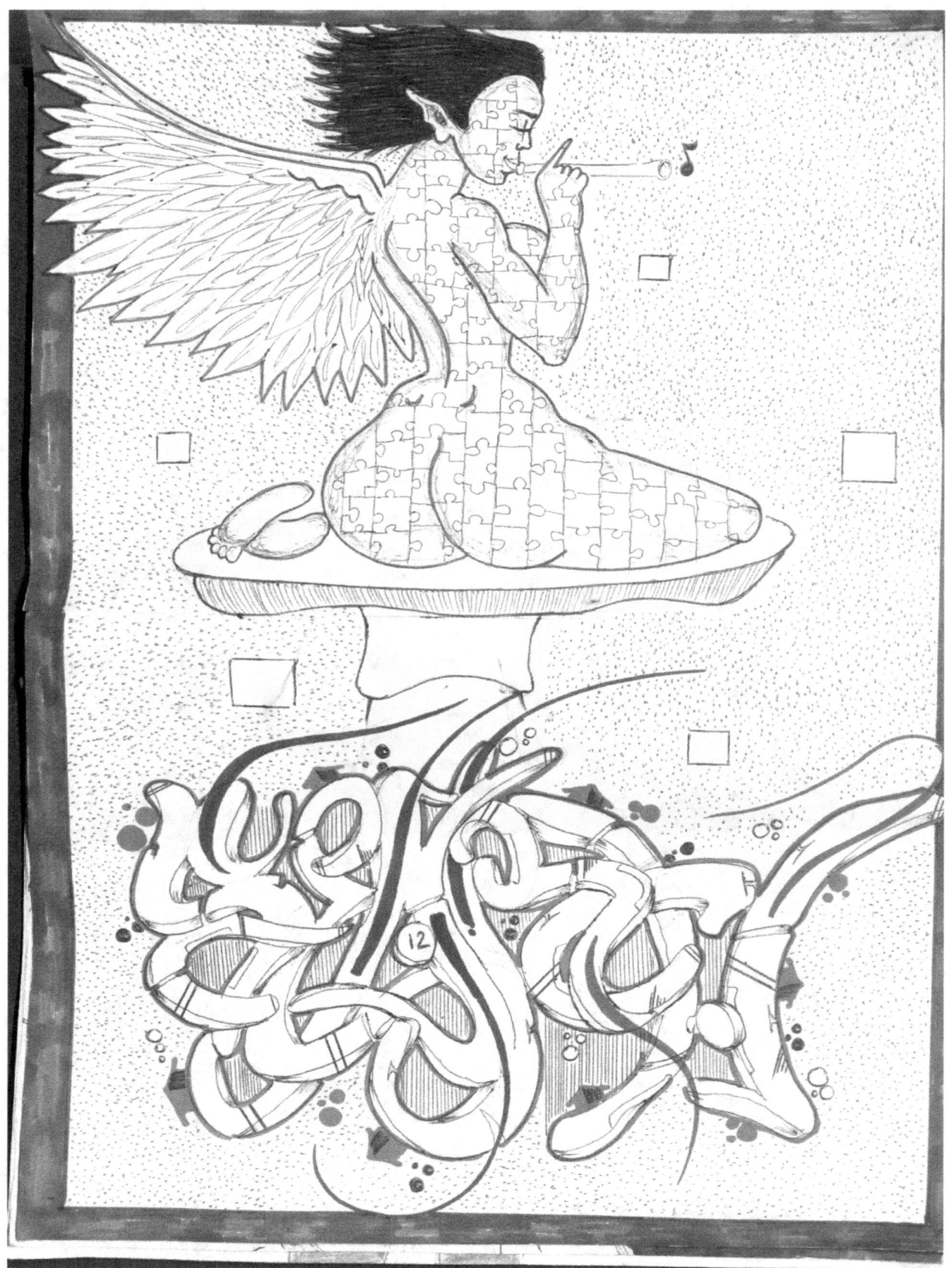

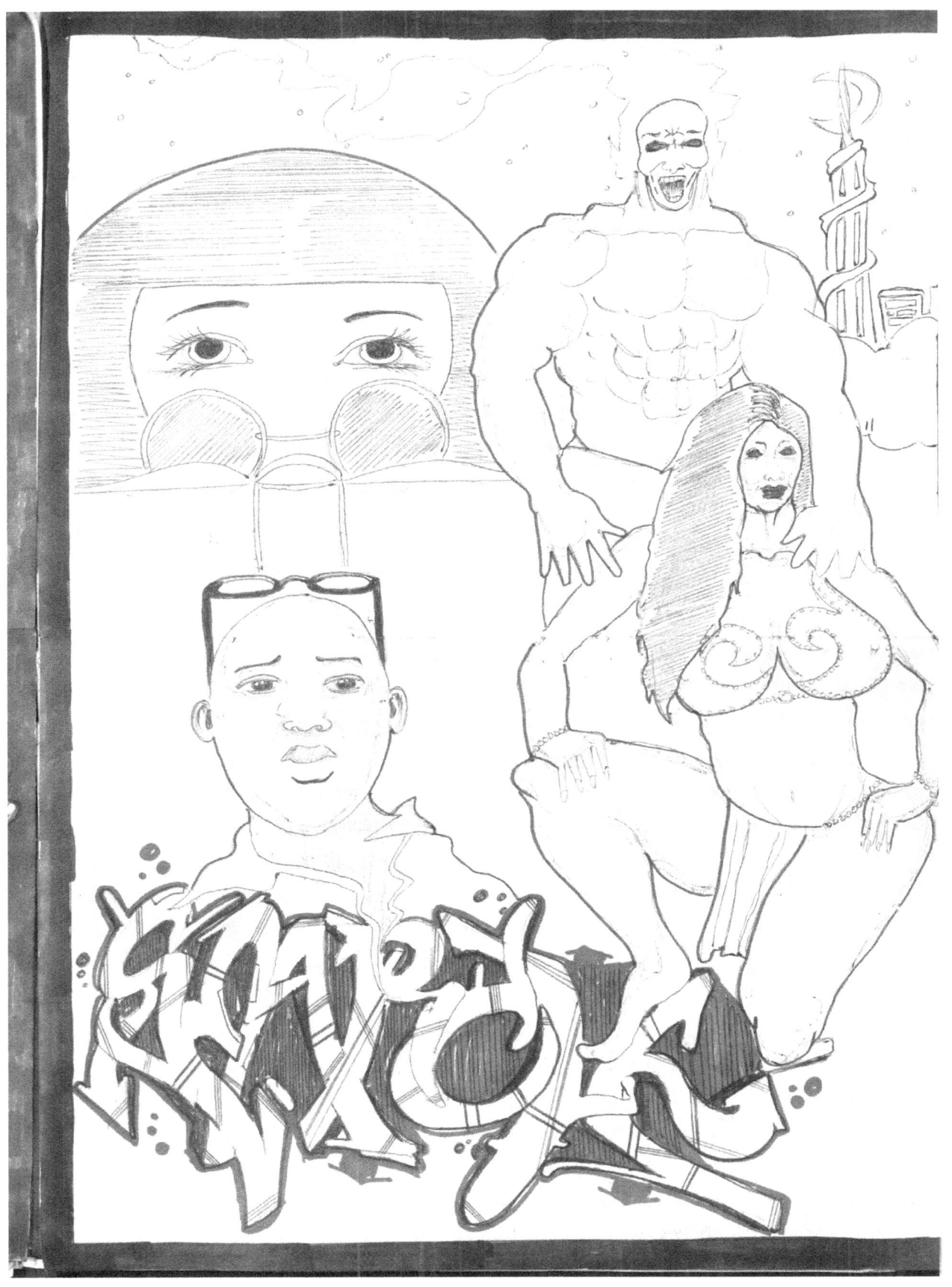

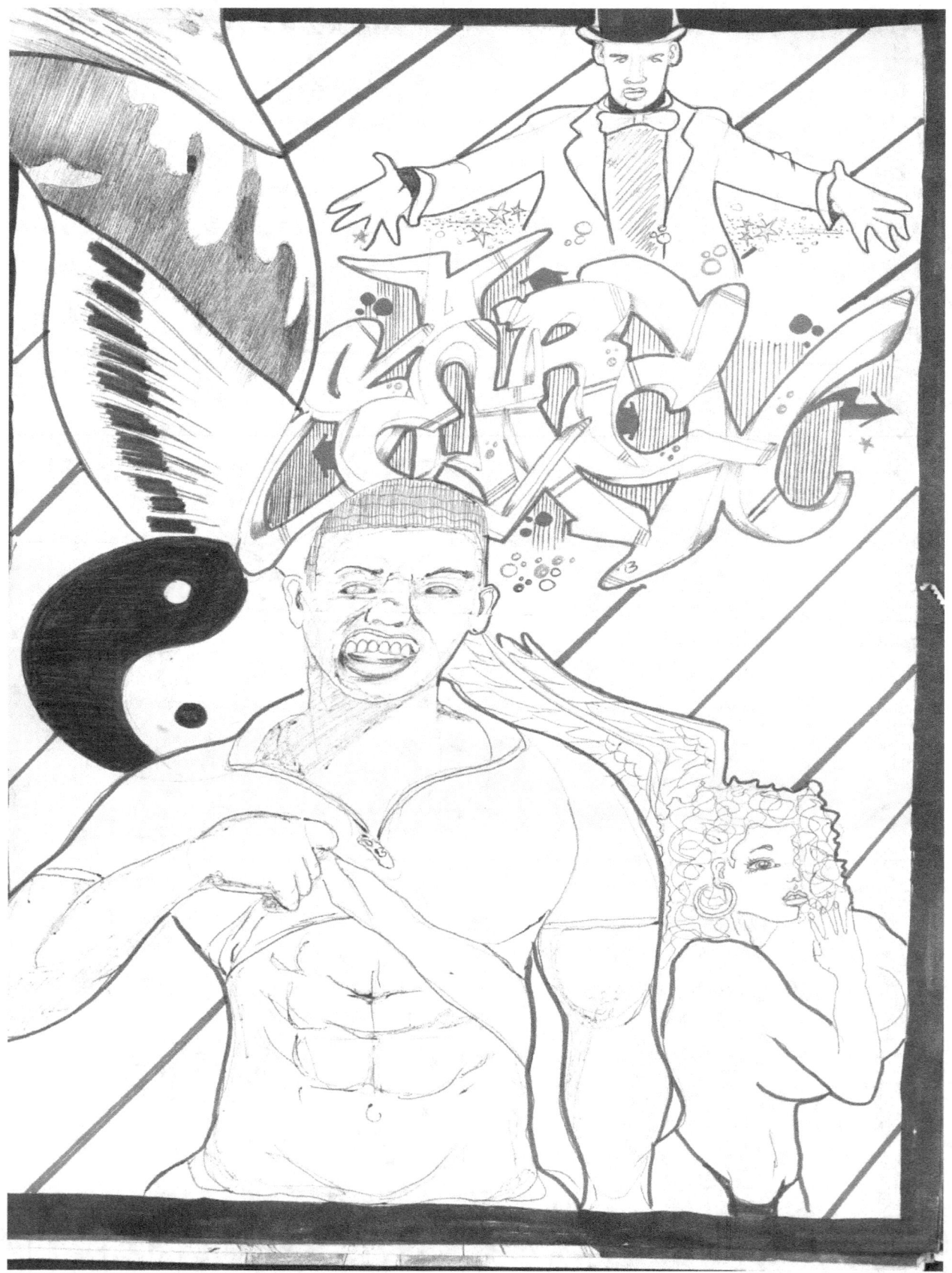

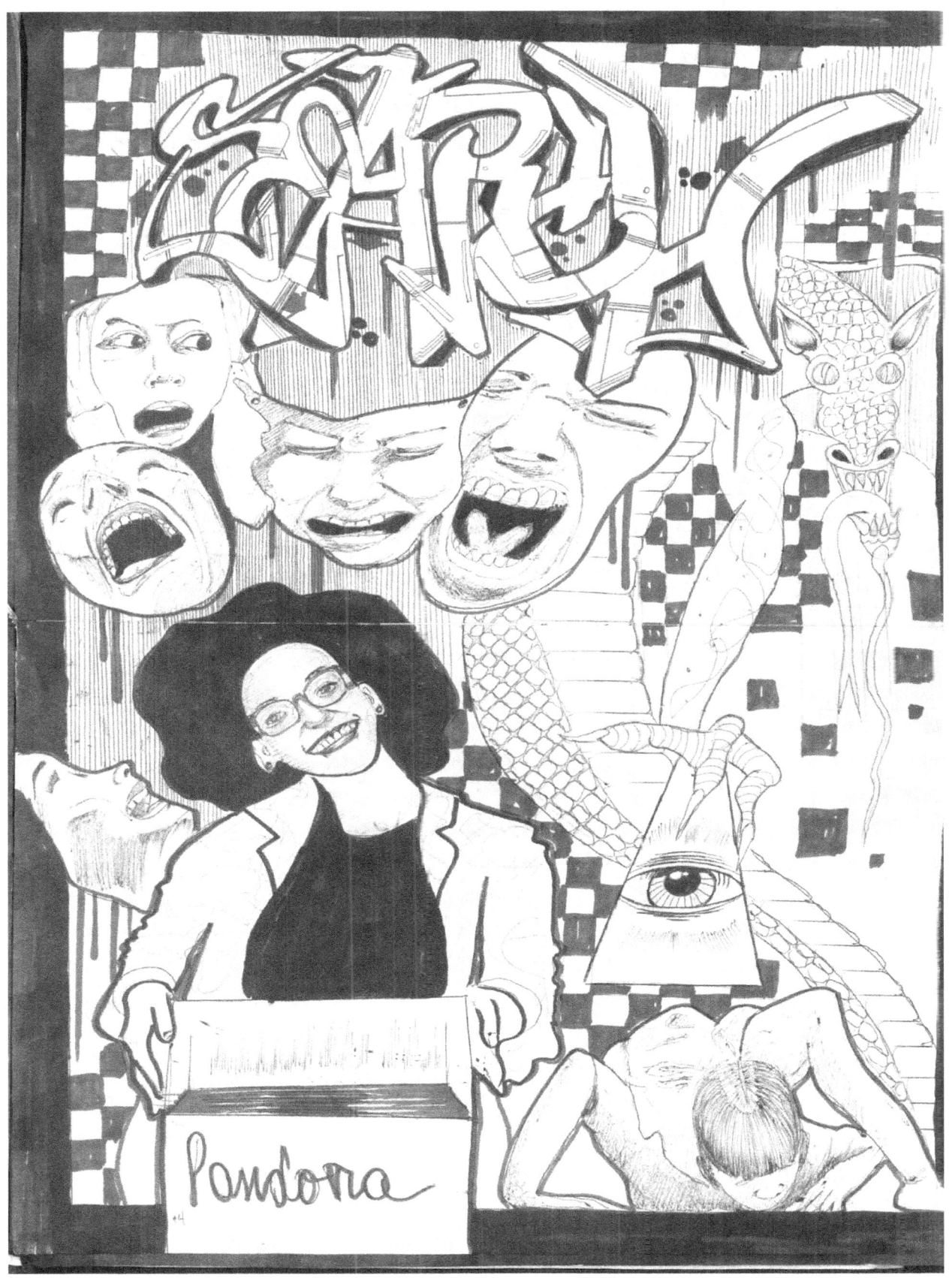

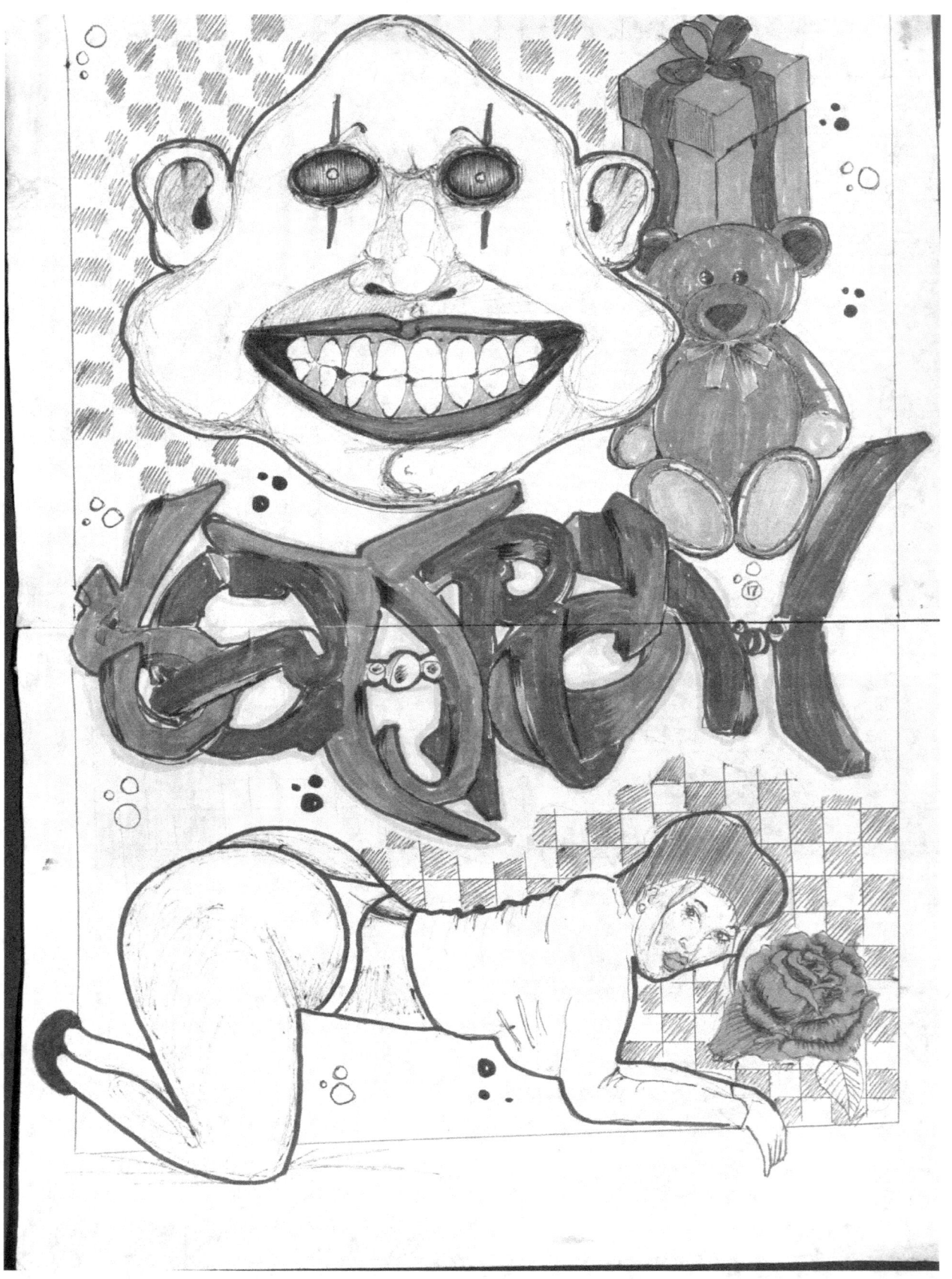

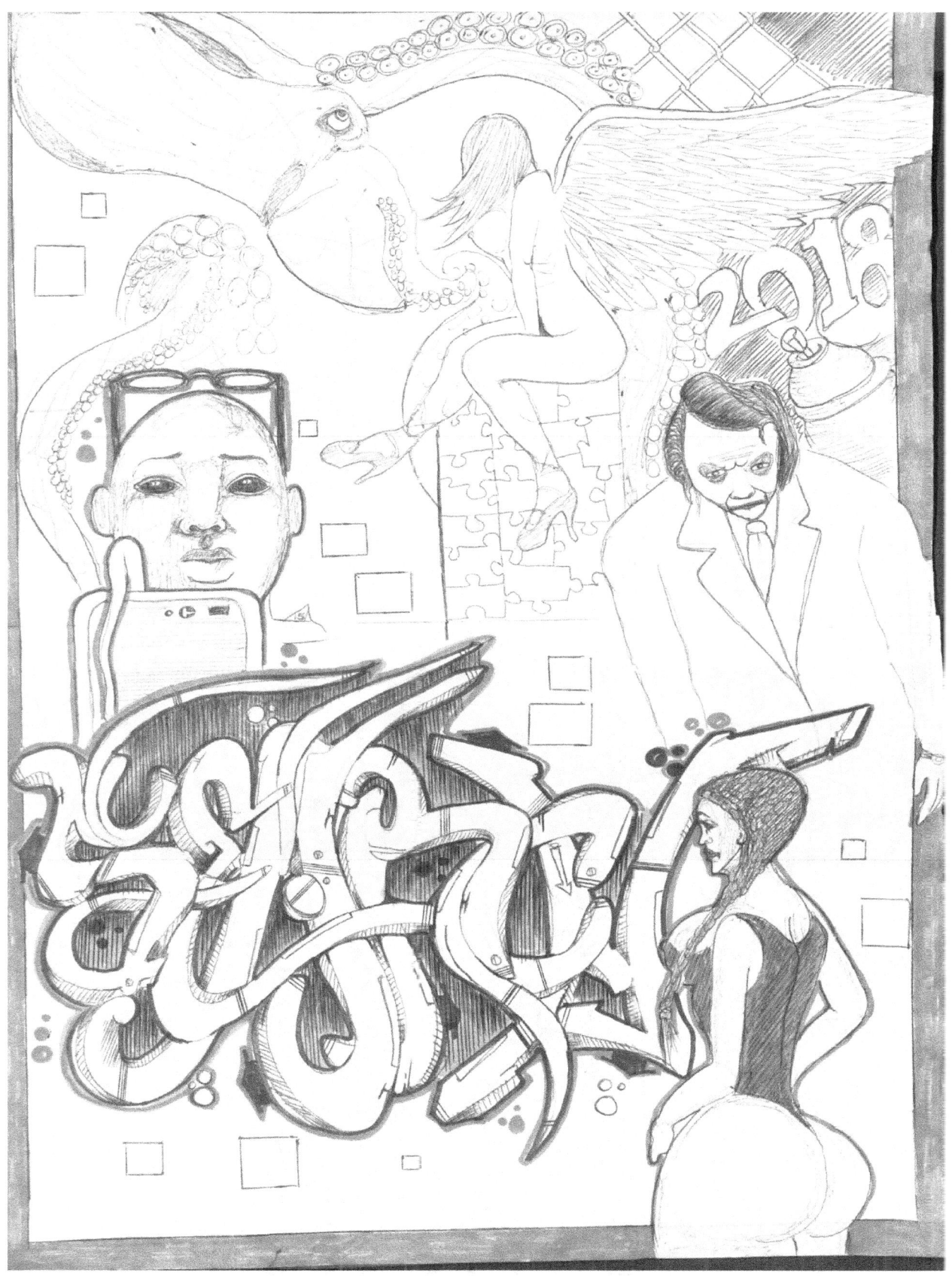

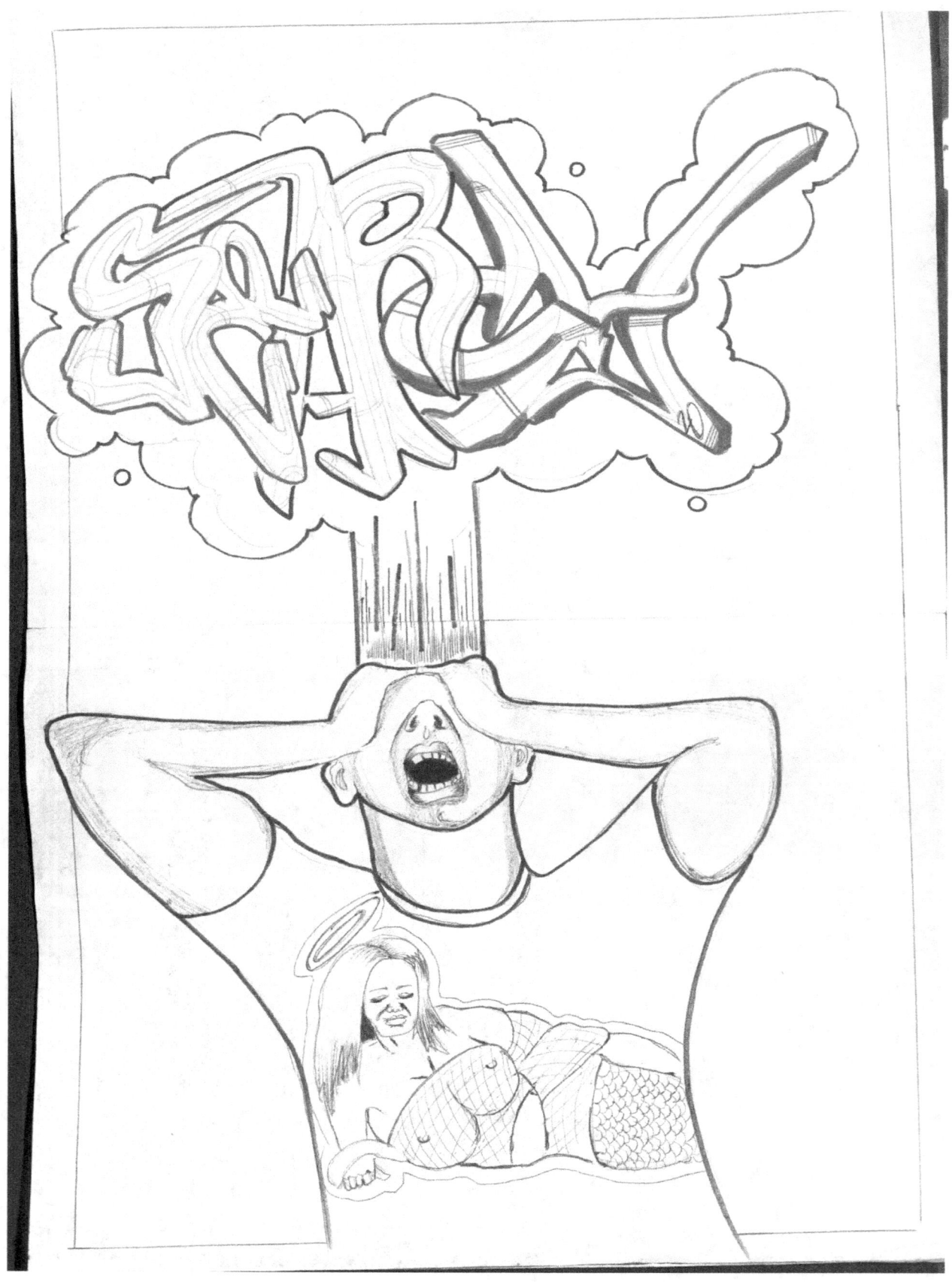

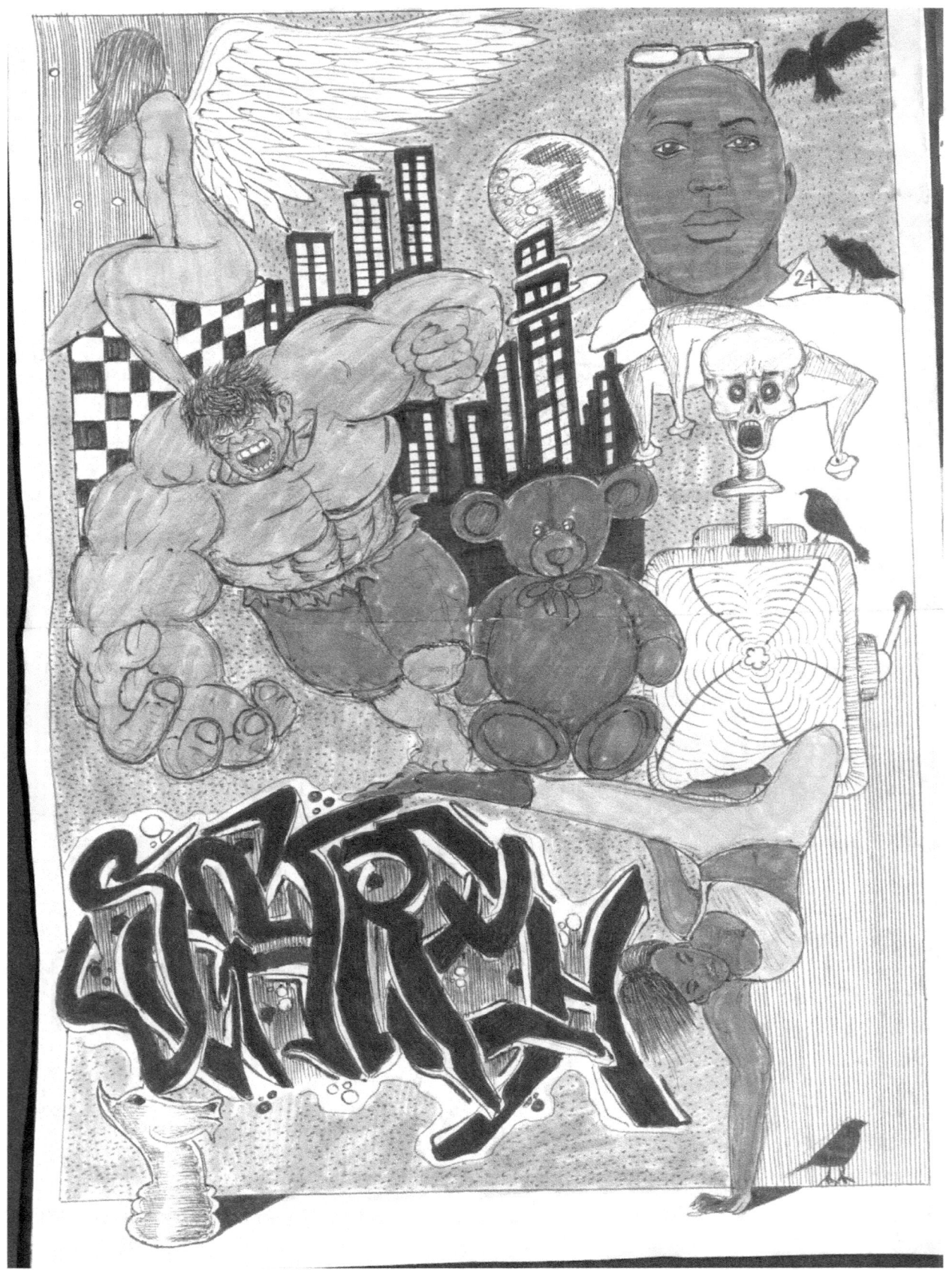

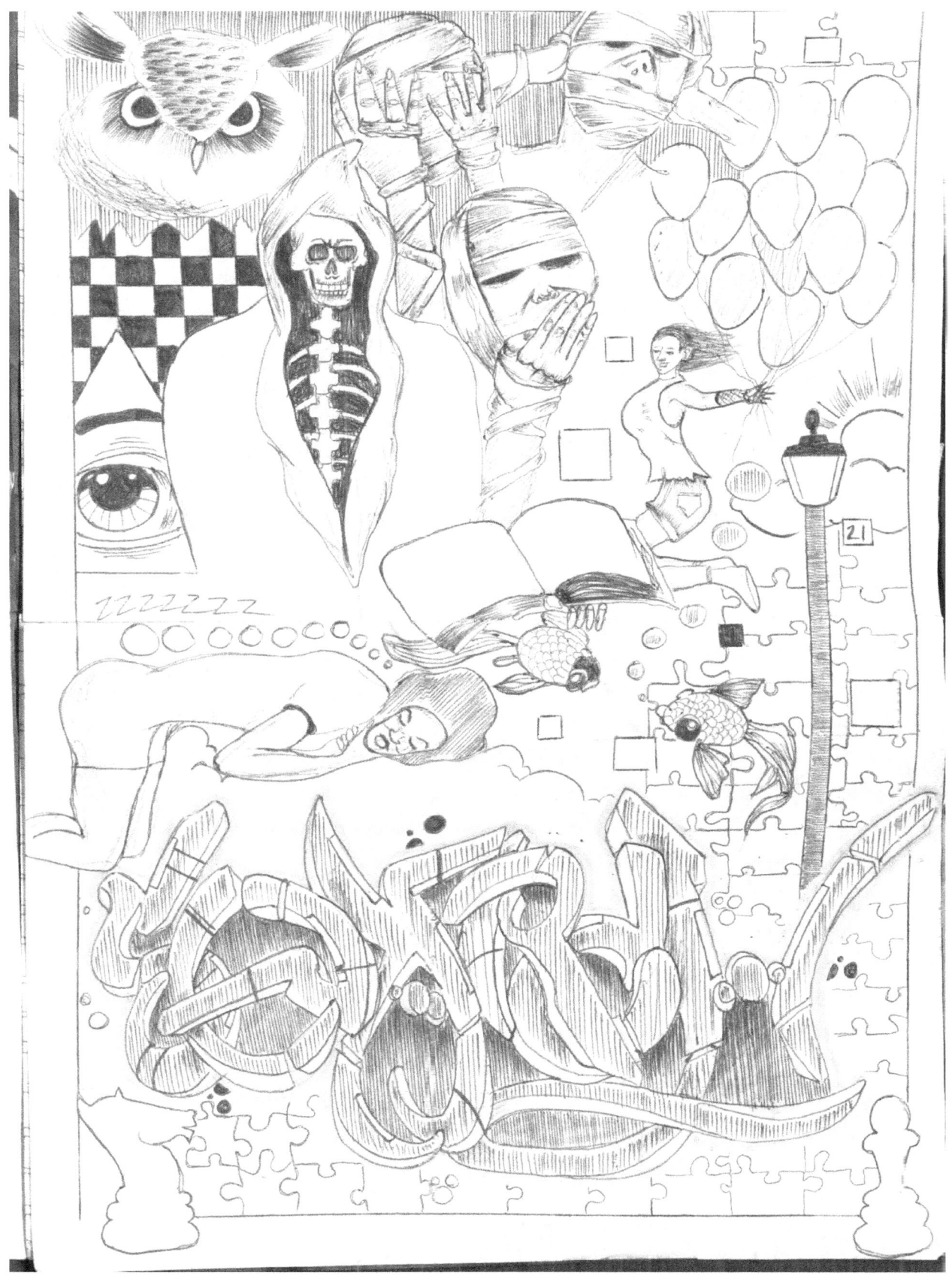

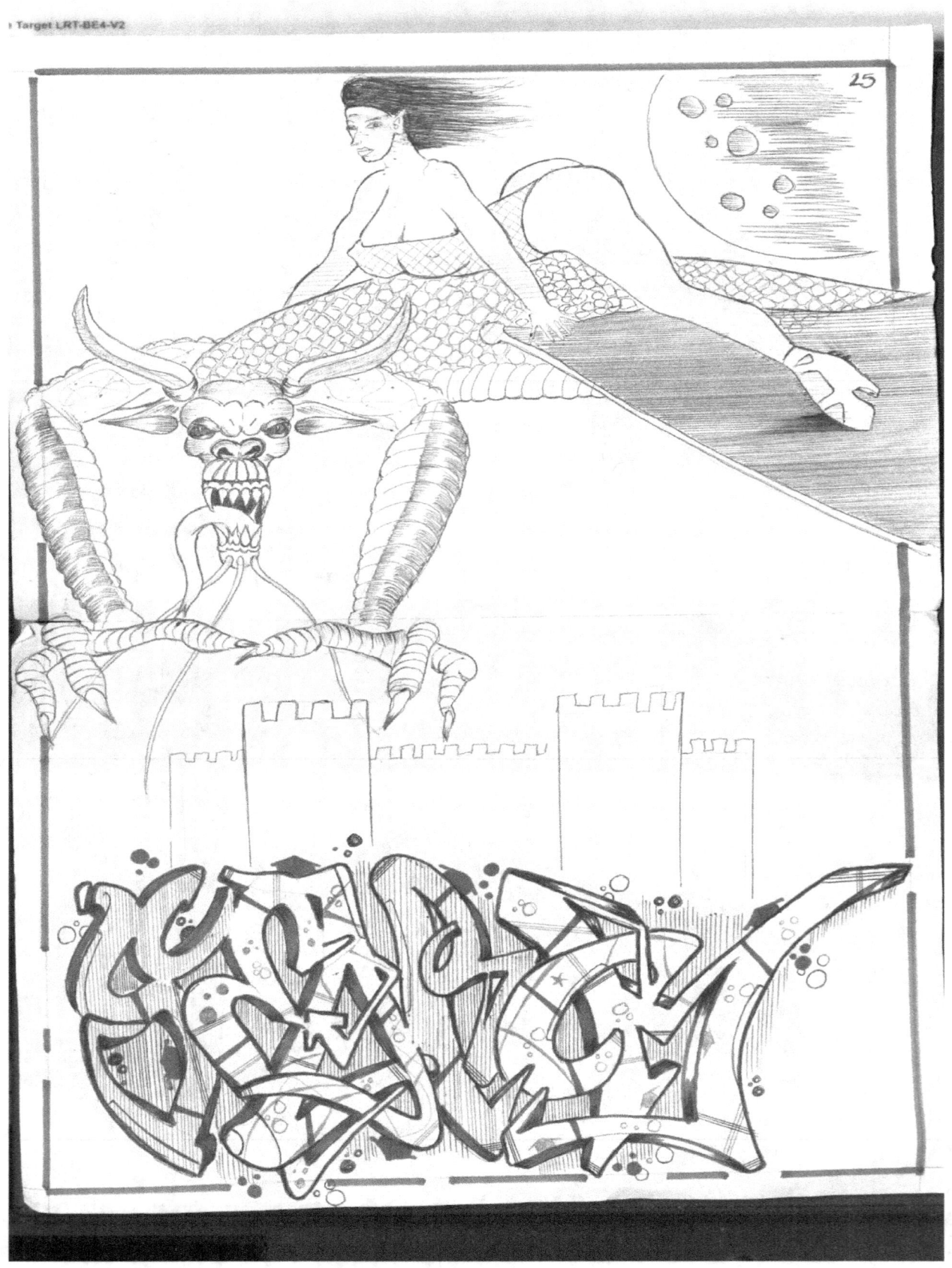

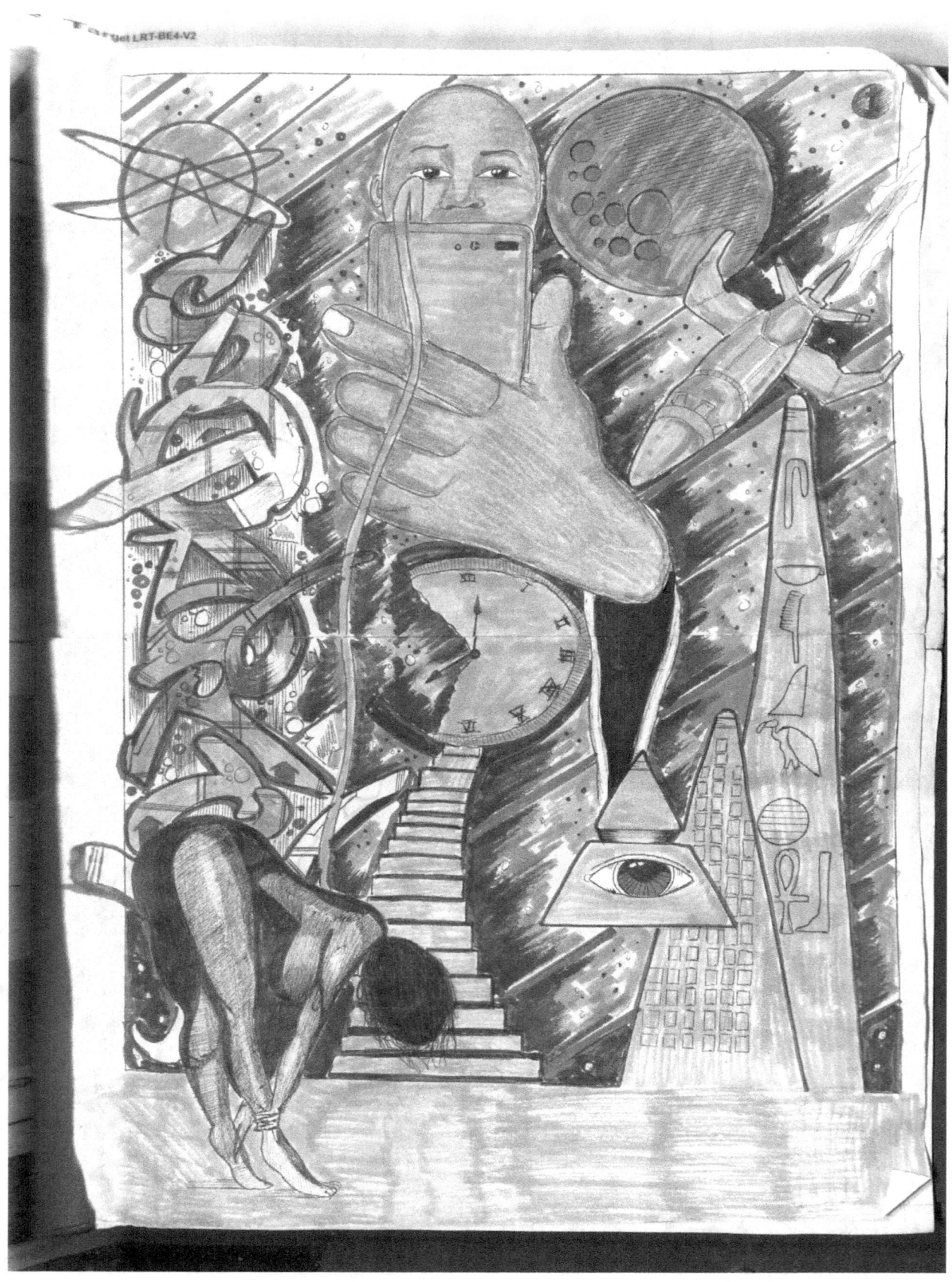

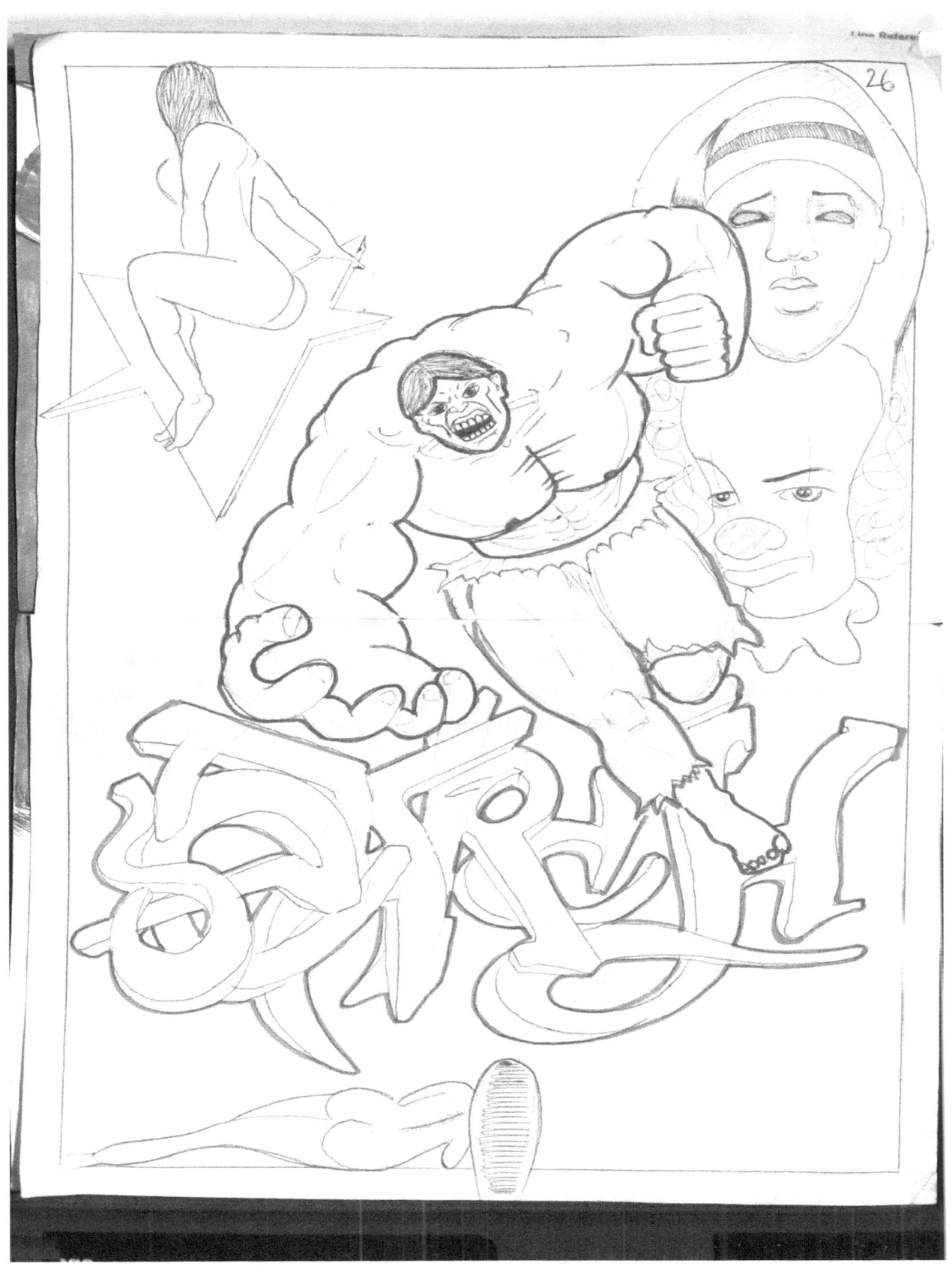

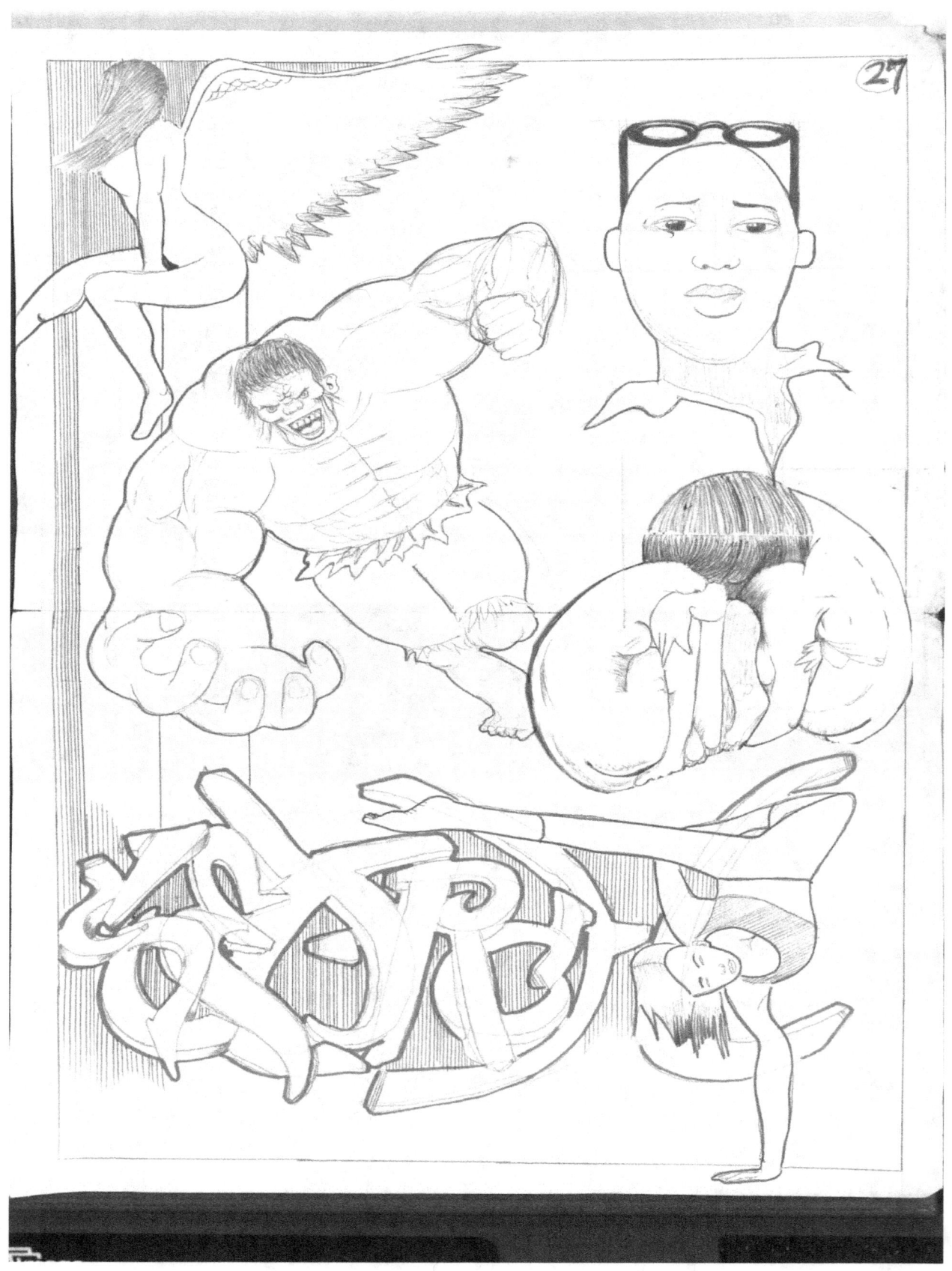

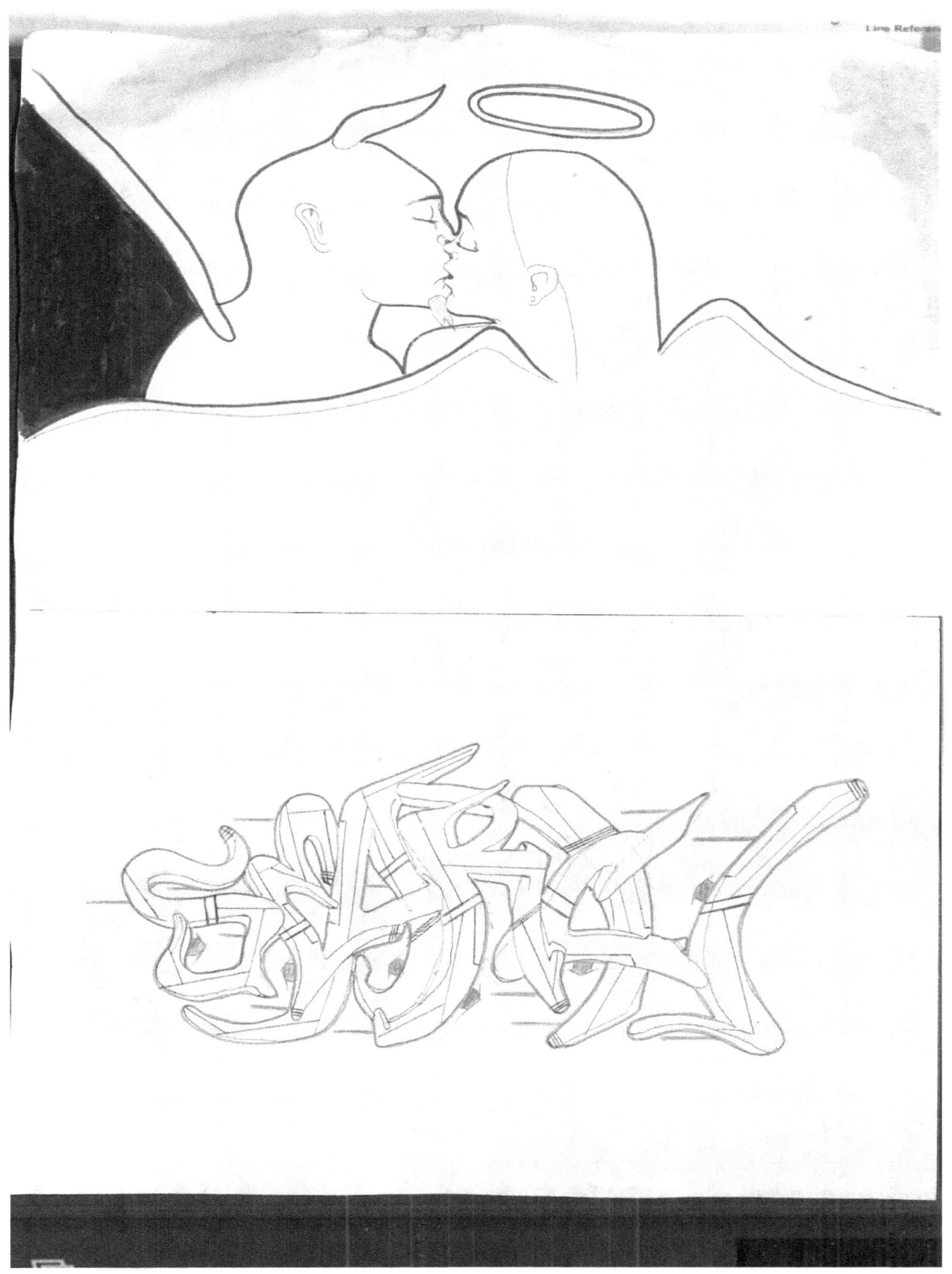

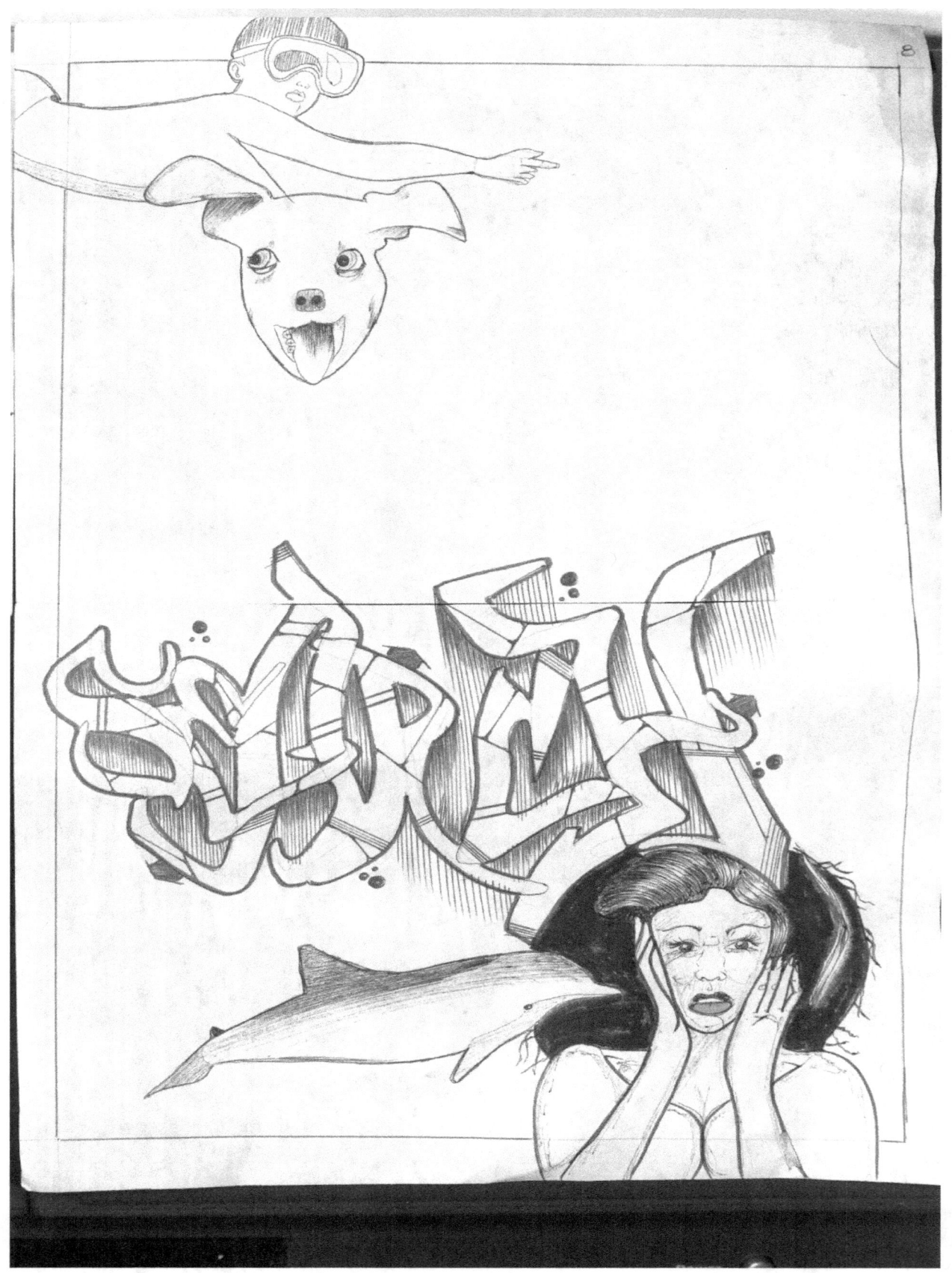

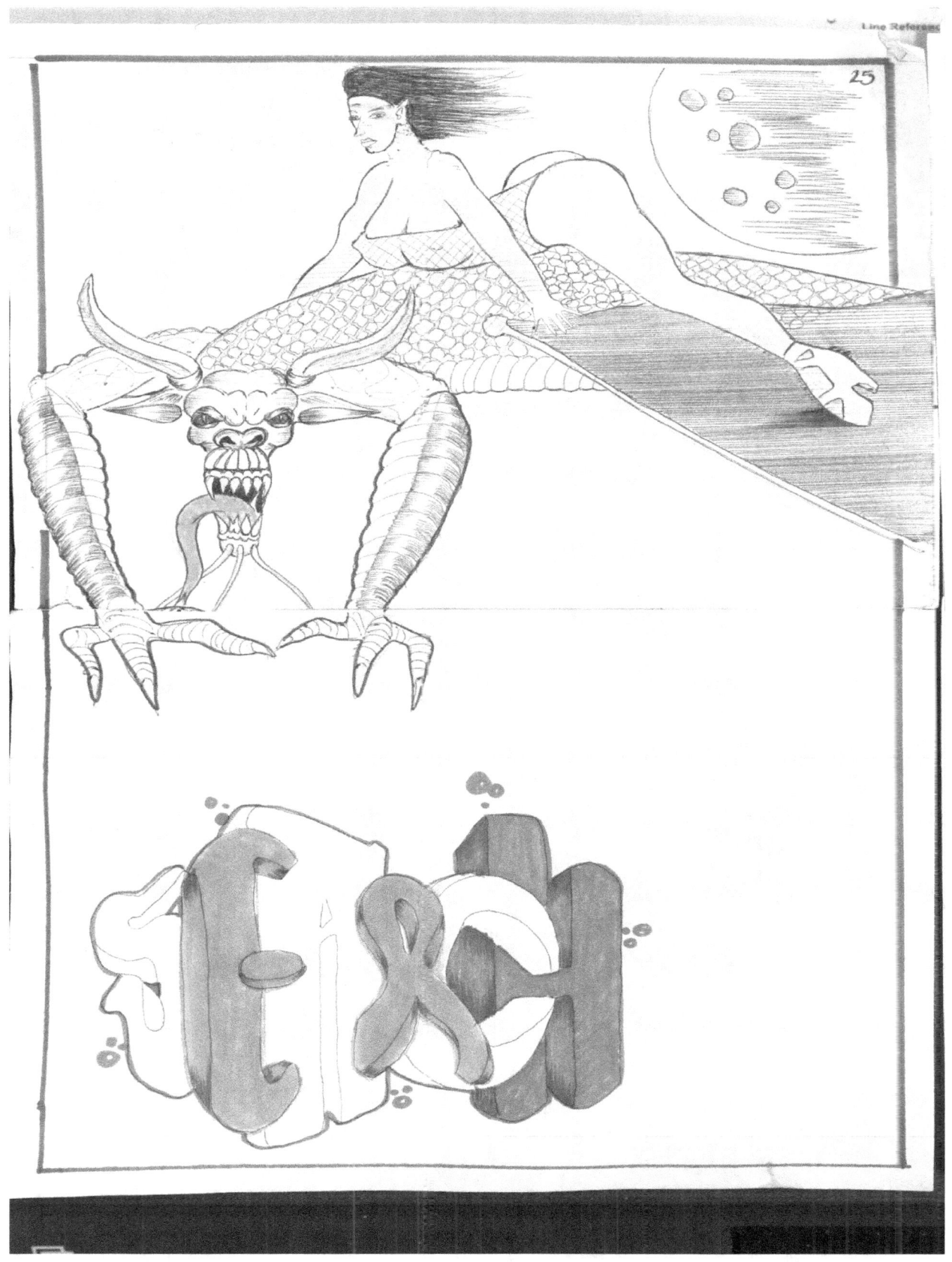

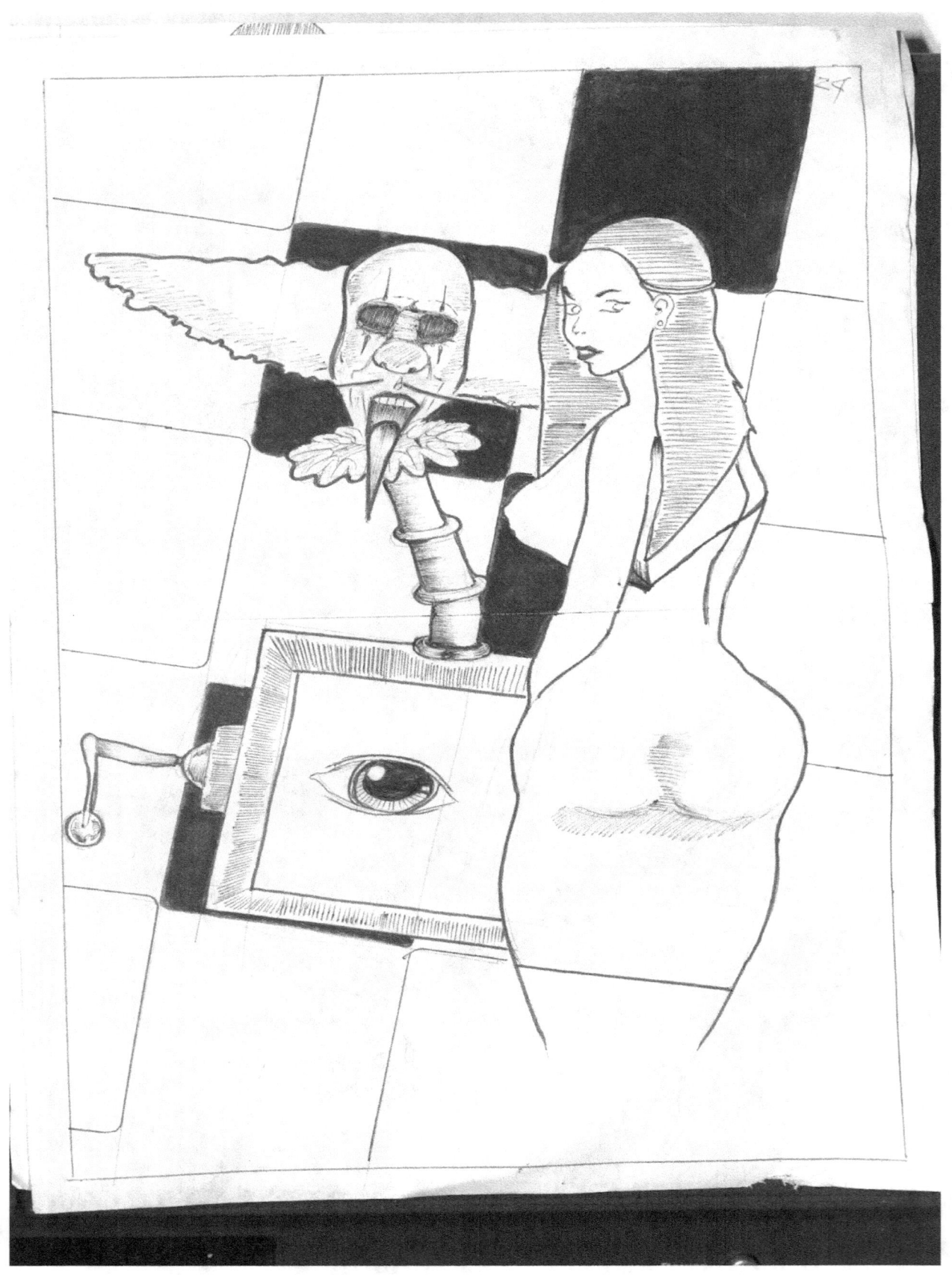

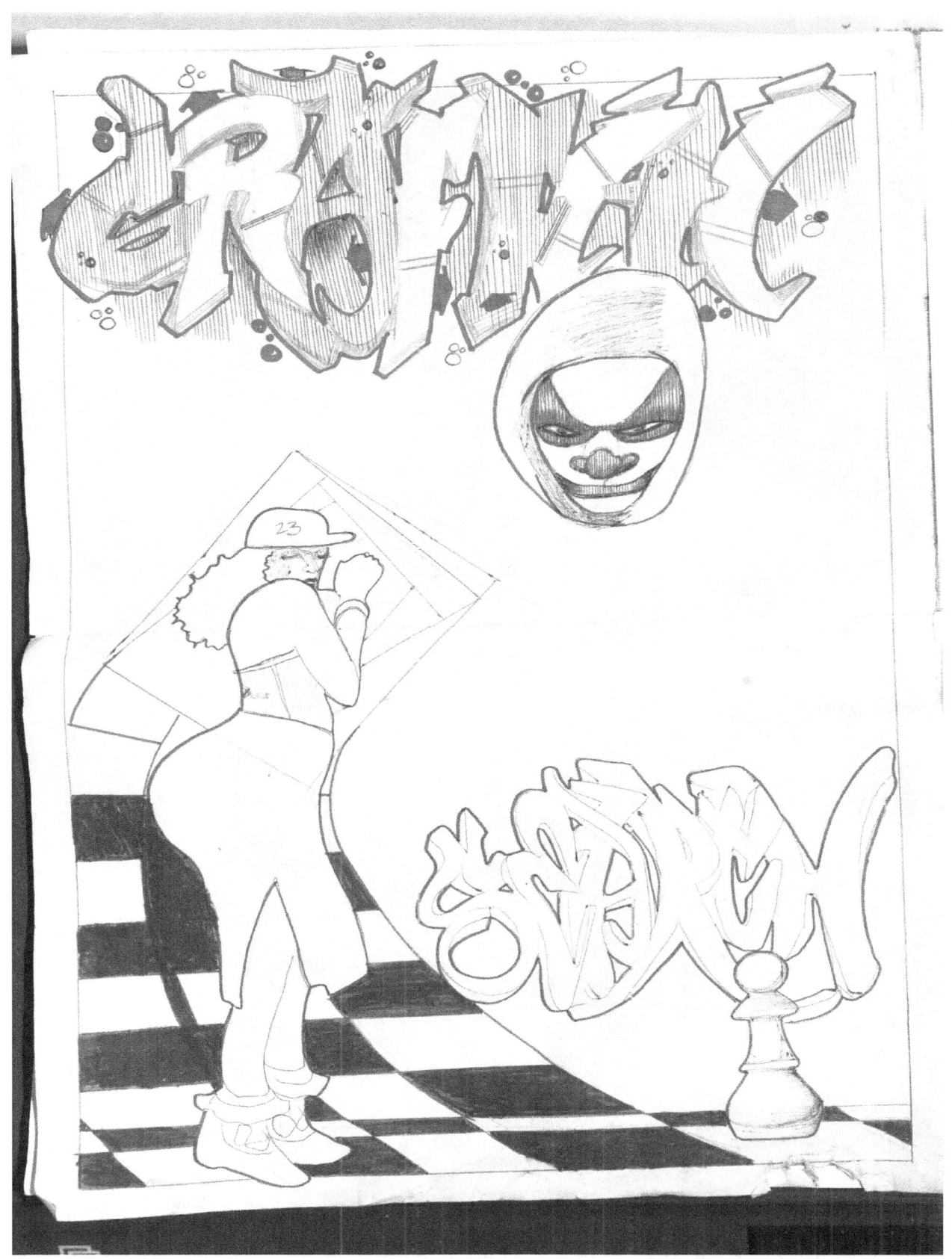

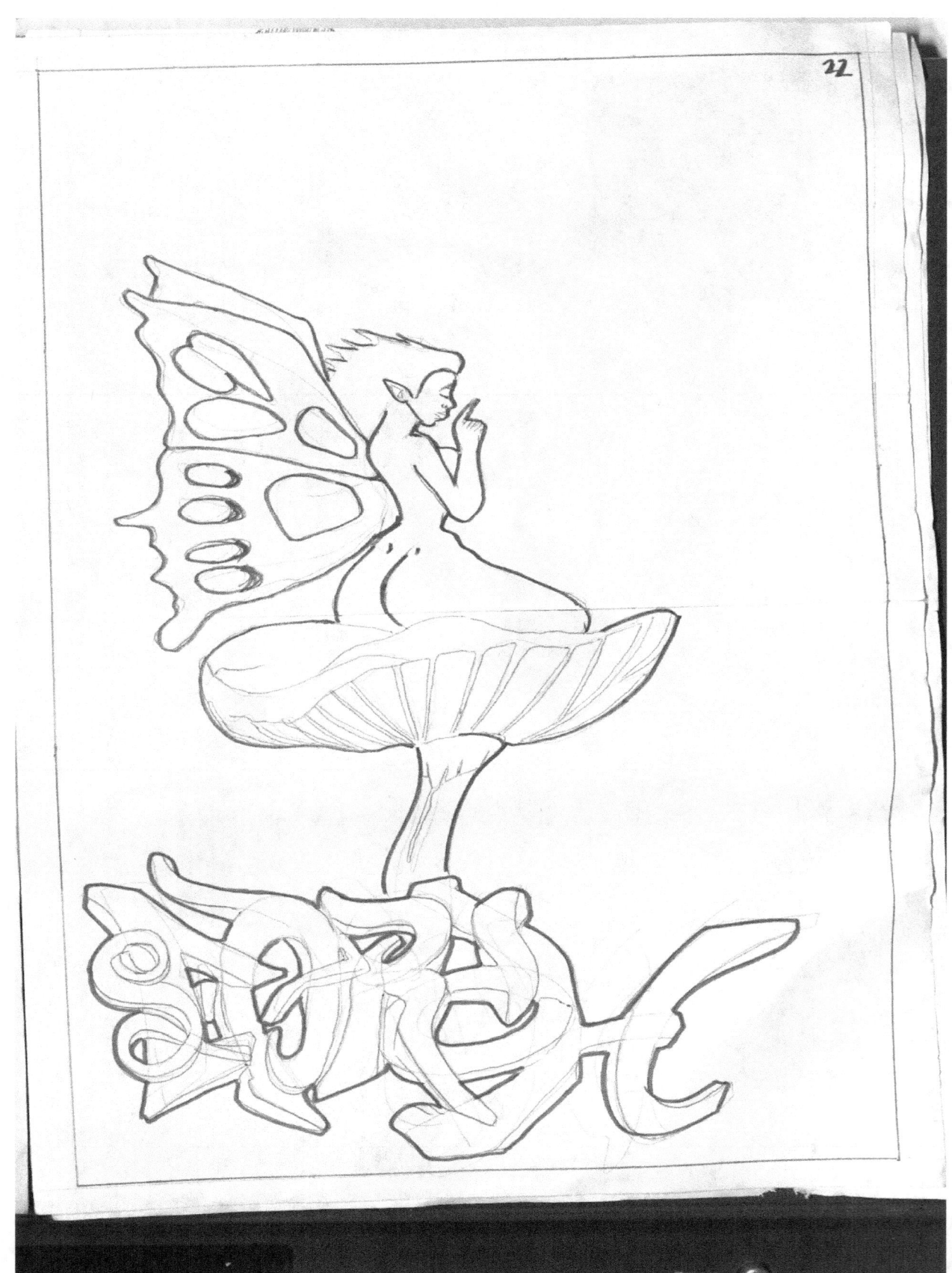

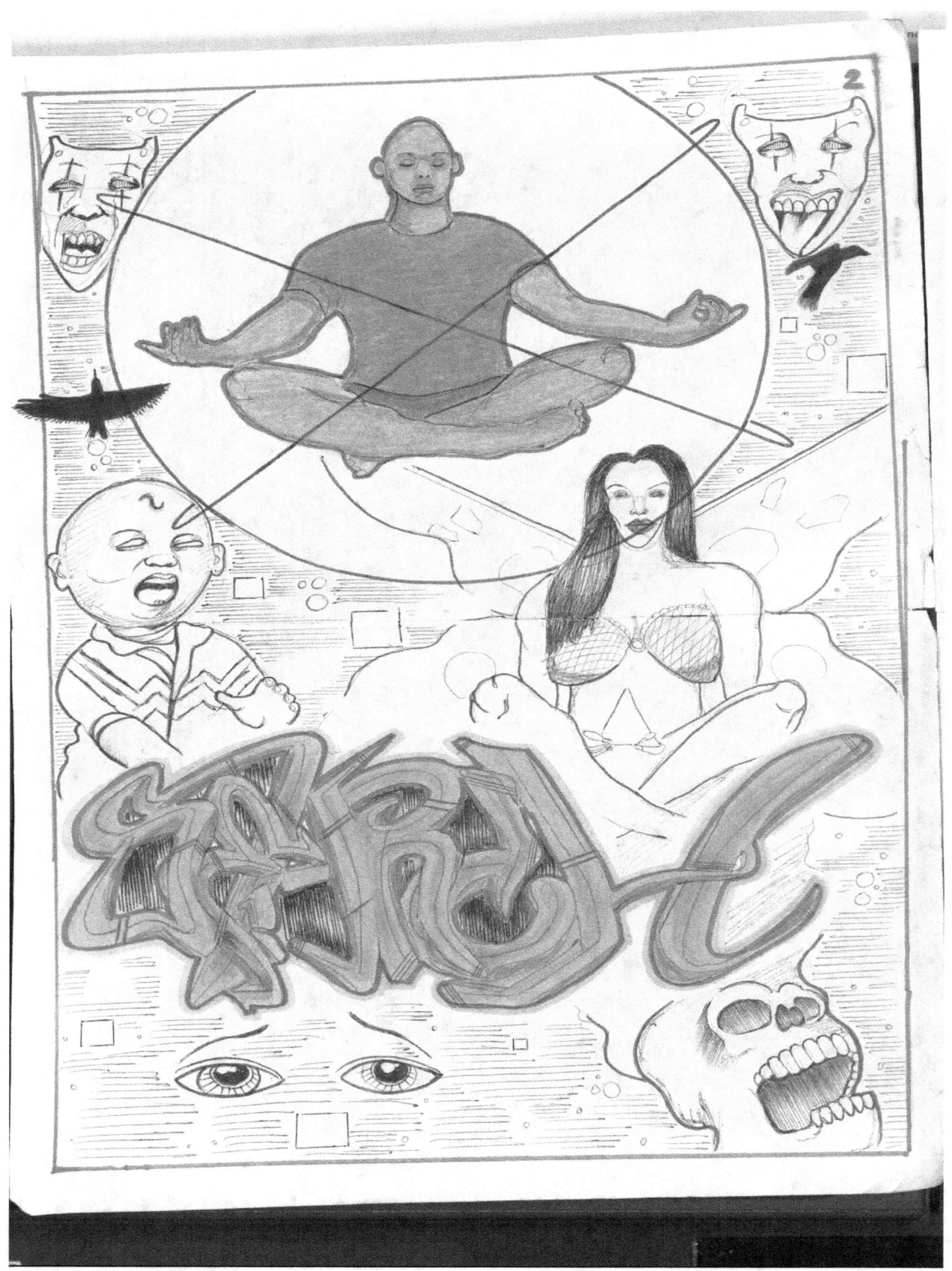

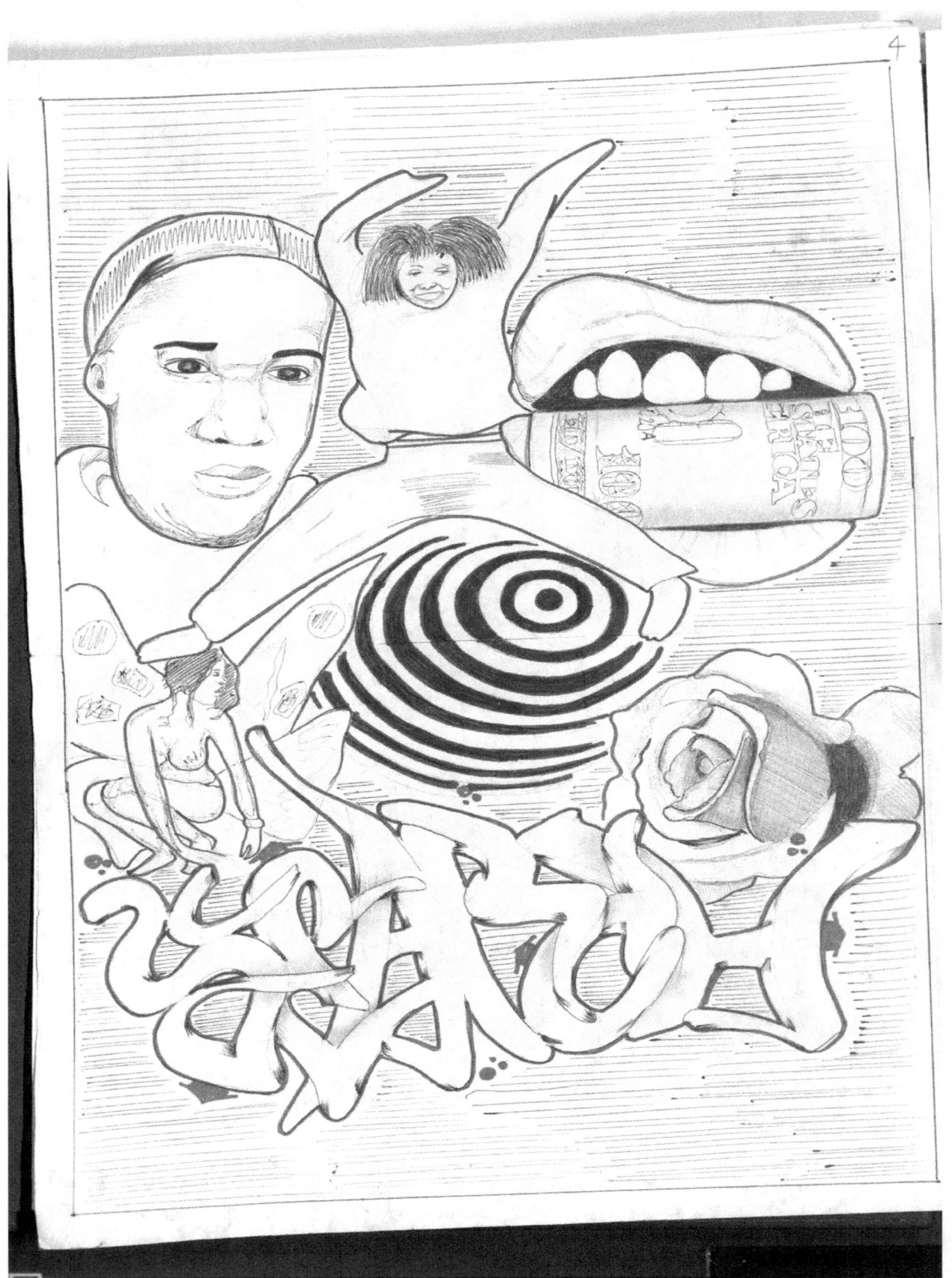

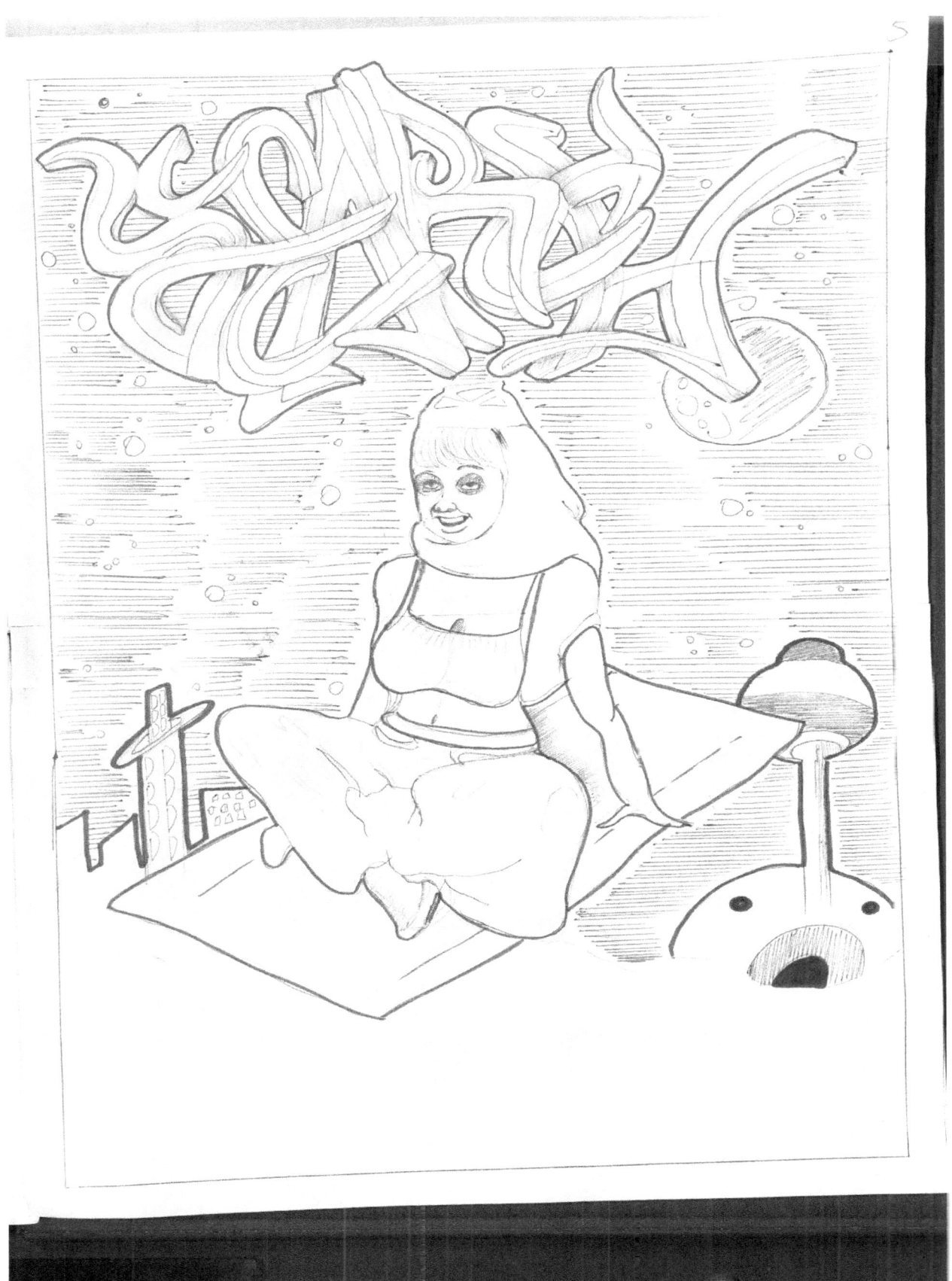

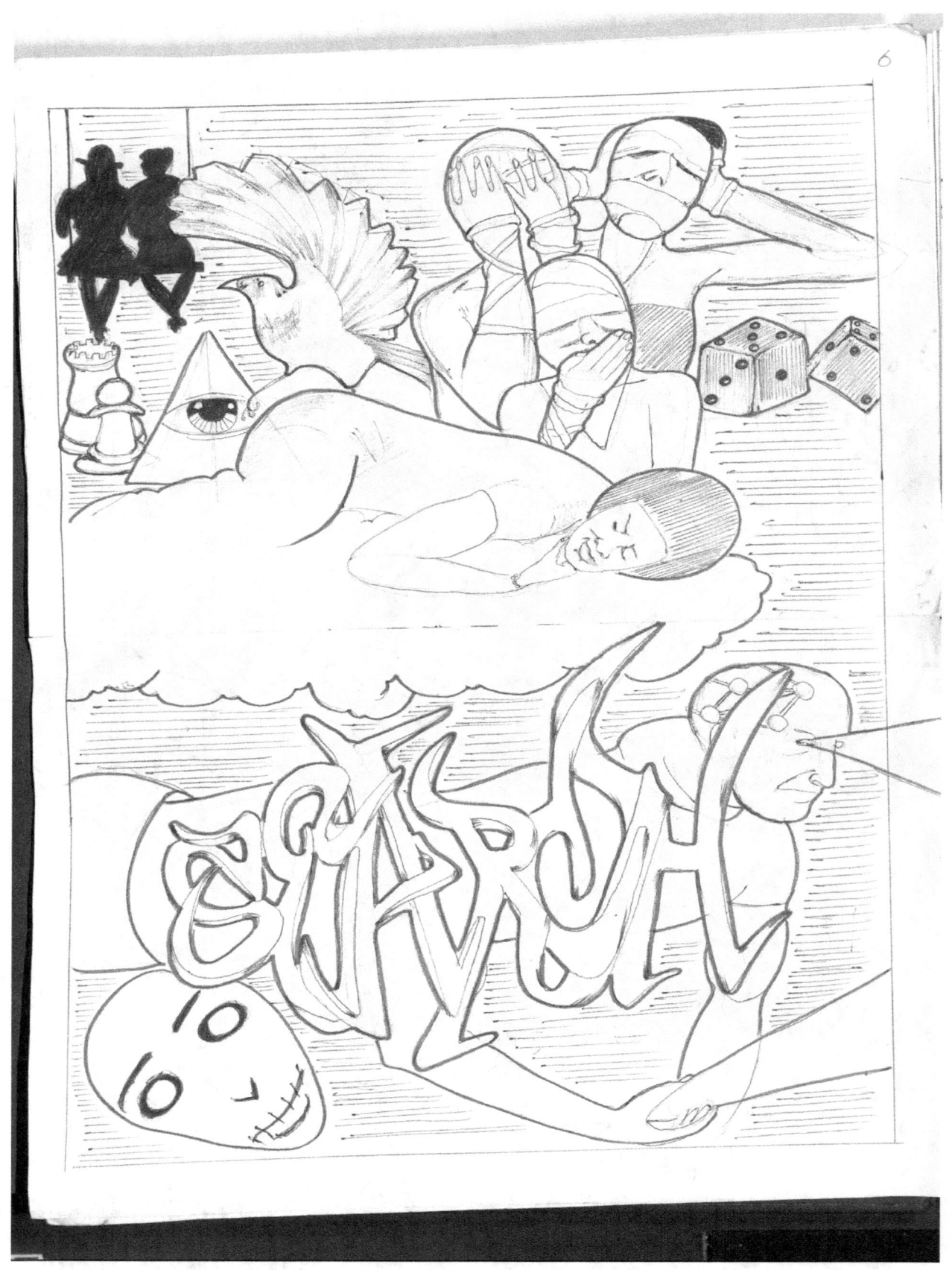

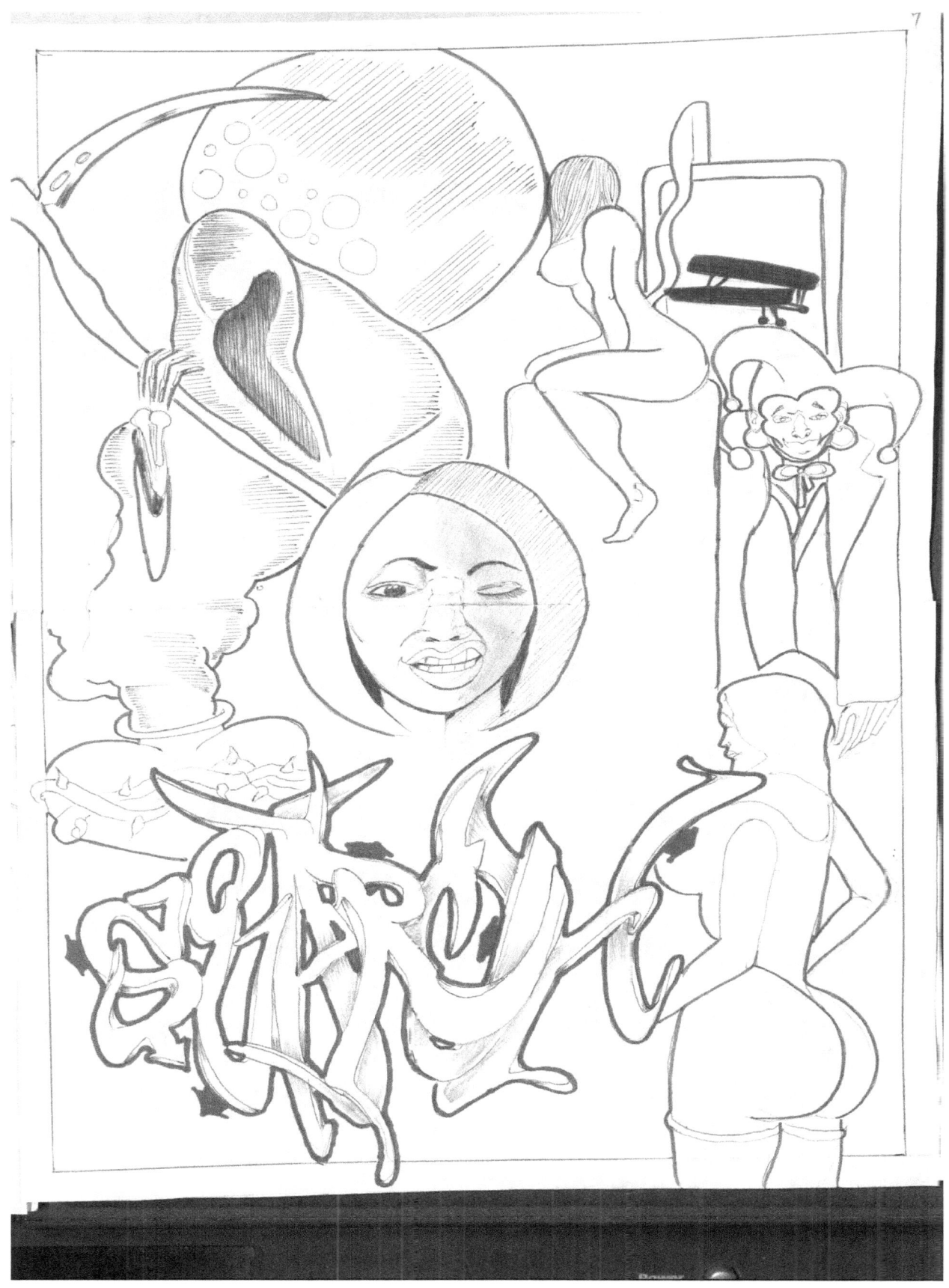

www.ingramcontent.com/pod-product-compliance
Lightning Source LLC
Chambersburg PA
CBHW082109220526
45472CB00009B/2113